THE PALESTINIAN MYSTERY PLAY

THE PALESTINIAN MYSTERY PLAY

Based on *The Shining Stranger* by Preston Harold

by Winifred Babcock

A HAROLD INSTITUTE BOOK

DISTRIBUTED BY DODD, MEAD & COMPANY

NEW YORK

THE PALESTINIAN MYSTERY PLAY appears as Book I of THE SINGLE REALITY by Preston Harold and Winifred Babcock. Book II introduces Harold's theory of the living universe, and Book III contains the remainder of his manuscripts that present his hypothesis regarding the nature of energy and the way it communicates.

DODD, MEAD & COMPANY, New York and Toronto, distributes the books of
Preston Harold to the trade. Bookstores may order from:
Dodd, Mead & Co., Inc.
79 Madison Avenue
New York, New York 10016

Individuals may order Harold's books from HAROLD INSTITUTE if local book-
stores do not stock them. Send order and check to:
Harold Institute
P. O. Box 11024
Winston-Salem, North Carolina 27106

The following Harold books are available:

THE SHINING STRANGER by Preston Harold, Introduction by Gerald Heard
Hardcover: $7.50 plus 50¢ mailing charges
Paperback: $1.95 plus 50¢ mailing charges

A SYNOPSIS OF THE SHINING STRANGER by Winifred Babcock
Pamphlet — 40 pages. Single copy: $1.00 postpaid
Four or more copies: 50¢ each postpaid

THE SINGLE REALITY by Preston Harold and Winifred Babcock
Introduction and Summary by Oliver L. Reiser
Preface for the Physical Scientist by Robert M. L. Baker, Jr.
Hardcover: $7.95 plus 50¢ mailing charges

THE PALESTINIAN MYSTERY PLAY by Winifred Babcock*
Introduction by Oliver L. Reiser
Preface by Robert M. L. Baker, Jr.
Paperback: $2.95 plus 50¢ mailing charges

*THE PALESTINIAN MYSTERY PLAY also appears as Book I of THE SINGLE
REALITY

3-87

ISBN 0-396-06201-6
Library of Congress Catalog Card Number: 71-121986
Printed in the United States of America
by Vail-Ballou Press, Inc., Binghamton, N.Y.

To Charlie
Ed, Walter, Liza, and Janie

Only they know how much they have done
to make this book possible

EXCERPTS FROM ROBERT M. L. BAKER, JR.'S PREFACE FOR THE PHYSICAL SCIENTIST
THE SINGLE REALITY

Essentially, I view the philosophy of "Harold" as a description of the gradual evolution of the Universe from its absolutely inanimate physical conception to its absolutely animate biological conclusion. As the measure of physical disorder, entropy, inexorably increases, so also the measure of biological orderliness and sophistication ("syntropy") increases. The physical universe subsides in relevance while the "life" aspects of the Cosmos abound ever more fully, finally becoming the exclusive characterization of the Universe. The fascination of this process lies in the fact that the "life" aspects of the Universe must rely upon purely physical processes for their support and development. This suggests that this physical-principle cradle of "life" (i.e., the laws governing physical processes) may itself exhibit characteristics that are ordinarily attributed exclusively to life forms, e.g., love, hate, affection, etc. It is a bit far out, but some rather convincing arguments are included in this book.

•

Dr. Baker has been the editor of the *Journal of the Astronautical Sciences* since 1963. He was the joint editor of the *Proceedings* of the 1961 International Astronautical Federation Congress and the senior author of the first textbook on astrodynamics: *An Introduction to Astrodynamics*, published in 1960. Dr. Baker is the author of four books and over seventy technical papers. He is a trustee of West Coast University, and is on the Faculty of the Department of Engineering at UCLA.

EXCERPTS FROM OLIVER L. REISER'S INTRODUCTION TO THE SINGLE REALITY

By this time it is abundantly clear that Preston Harold's relentless efforts at synthesis represent his impressive contribution to the reconciliation and integration of scientific and religious motivations, attitudes, and achievements. His deep and sustained research toward this end is one of the great monuments to the spirit of man.

My response to the challenge of Harold's unique and novel philosophy of religion and science is that—beyond all doubt—it is worthy of concentrated and prolonged study. This clearly does not mean that the reader must agree with all, or even most, of what is set forth. For, as Gerald Heard has pointed out, one must only believe that it has sufficient merit to warrant publication and serious study. The validity of that judgment, I take it, is beyond question.

Harold's philosophy is capable of further developments, and finality is not claimed or expected. His synthesis generates excitement about the new findings of the "knowledge explosion" in all areas of science and religion and the arts. This is why his "unfinished symphony" is captivating. *The Palestinian Mystery Play* is still open-ended. Let us see what happens.

But first, because there will be many references to Cosmic Humanism as the play unfolds, a word about what Cosmic Humanism is will clarify the concept for the reader.

Cosmic Humanism is the name we give to man's ongoing search for truth. By the word *Cosmic* we indicate immediately that our search for truth must range from nuclear physics to astronomy, involving all the exact sciences. By the word *Humanism* we indicate that we must also search for truth through the whole range of life sciences, history, psychology, the arts, and the religious expressions of mankind.

Cosmic Humanism seeks to provide the framework within which scientific investigation of nature and the psyche of man can proceed in harmony with religious expression to lead man nearer to an understanding of his own being and of his Cosmic environment.

There is presently at hand sufficient evidence to allow us to transcend both the nihilism of materialistic philosophy and the fragmented exclusiveness of the world's authoritarian religions.

The search for synthesis must be inward into the psyche of man, and outward—from elementary particles to the furthest reaches of Cosmic space that technology and the mind of Homo sapiens can reach. Action on the social scene will reflect what man believes about himself, the universe, and his place in it. An enhanced and ennobled image of man will lead to an age of peace on earth, respect for every human being, and the development of a society conducive to the development of the human potential. A cosmology that affirms the creative principle inherent in universal operation will lead to a release of the creative capacities in man.

Toward this end, Cosmic Humanism focuses.

•

Oliver L. Reiser has published numerous books on his "philosophical journey" which culminates momentarily in *Cosmic Humanism*. Albert Einstein, referring to *World Philosophy: A Search for Synthesis*, comments that Reiser "has overcome, without sacrificing his intellectual integrity, the paralyzing relativism that so many clear thinkers of our times feel themselves forced to accept." The *Annals of the American Academy* refers to this same book as "the most promising guide out of our present world of chaos and confusion."

Dr. Reiser was formerly chairman of the Philosophy Department of the University of Pittsburgh. Upon the occasion of his becoming Professor Emeritus, the A. W. Mellon Educational and Charitable Trust awarded him a fellowship for his next major undertaking, the research and writing of a book entitled *Magnetic Moments in Human History*.

Dr. Reiser is presently chairman of The Committee for Cosmic Humanism.

THE PALESTINIAN MYSTERY PLAY

ACT ONE

Setting the Stage for *The Shining Stranger*

Prologue

Preston Harold is a pen name. No one connected with publishing the Harold papers knows who or what the author was. We were informed that he is deceased, and we are confident that his identity can never be made known. Extraordinary precautions were taken to insure this. In accordance with the unknown author's instructions, all copies of his manuscripts have been destroyed in order to maintain his anonymity.

The new answer to the mystery of man, the mystery of Jesus, presented in *The Palestinian Mystery Play* is drawn from *The Shining Stranger*, by Preston Harold, with introduction by Gerald Heard,[4] and from Harold's hypothesis, *On the Nature of Universal Cross-Action*, which is being published as a part of this book, *The Single Reality*.

Although Gerald Heard sponsored *The Shining Stranger*, he did not commit himself to Harold's hypothesis regarding universal cross-action. Nor did he reject it. He did not feel himself sufficiently competent in physics to evaluate this work. Therefore, it was determined to publish it separately.

Harold's hypothesis was originally intended to be included with *The Shining Stranger*, and the whole volume was to be given the title *The Single Reality*, using the pen name of Mason M. Taylor for the unknown author. Difficulties arose. The book was too long, even after many passages that we felt to be essential to understanding the material were omitted. A few copies of the chapter dealing with the hypothesis on universal cross-action were printed and privately circulated to see what the reaction would be. It became apparent that both works would suffer if they were combined, and we concluded that they should be handled separately. A new pen name for the author was chosen, and the title for the first volume of his work was changed from *The Single Reality* to *The Shining Stranger*.

Much material was cut to reduce the original manuscript to manageable size. More was deleted when the two works were separated. I regretted the omission of a single sentence. As I typed and retyped the manuscript, certain passages to be struck impressed me deeply. I have drawn upon my memory to reconstitute them as best I can. It is difficult to separate what I remember of Harold's own words and my interpolations and interpretations. Because of this, we are coauthors of *The Single Reality*, which is more or less a paraphrasing of his published and unpublished work, except for Book III, *On the Nature of Universal Cross-Action*, in which the author speaks for himself, detailing his hypothesis.

Part of my job was to check the 1,241 references Harold gave to document his statements in *The Shining Stranger*. As Henry Miller commented, "the author's erudition is formidable. But anyone eager to get his 'message' will be able to read between the lines. . . ."[5]

I have read the lines many times and have also tried to read between the lines to capture the essence of the monumental synthesis Harold drew, bringing into harmonious relationship the religions of the world, the sciences, and psychology, the arts, and economy of humankind.

On the Nature of Universal Cross-Action is a hypothesis dealing with the constitution of elementary particles and the way energy communicates its forces. The hypothesis is a synthesis of astronomy and nuclear physics that provides a comprehensive theory of the living universe in which the wave-particle theory of light (a synthesis of the opposing theories) operates. The five major cosmogonies are synthesized and transcended to produce a cosmology that lifts science from the *cul de sac* of nihilism and affirms the never-ending ability of the Cosmos to engender and support life.

There is nothing mystical about Harold's work, but he left no mathematical formulas. This has been of great concern because physicists speak and listen only in mathematical terms. Mathematics is a shorthand, a concise method of presenting concepts that have the quality of encouraging the flow of logical thought. But words also have this quality, and they have the advantage of being understood by the mathematically uninitiated. Words, too, pose exquisite equations, as poetry does. I am neither physicist nor mathematician, but I fell in love with the subject as I read the books Harold draws upon. They made me so anxious to know more about every branch of physics that I can express my feelings only in the words of Oscar Wilde: "The anxiety is unbearable, and I hope it lasts forever."[6] Then a line from Harold's material, now lost in its original form, came to mind—anxiety attenuates and is recast as *interest*. He was referring to the evolution of consciousness as a process through which the destructive potential in life is reorganized in time and converts to something of value.

Regardless of the response accorded Harold's work by the scientific world, I believe it has great value because of his ability to create interest in science, and his approach to it helps to bridge the "two cultures" that now stand divided.

Of equal importance is Harold's synthesis of religions, which provides a basis for true reconciliation and unity among them—although the integrity and individual approach of each is supported. He centers attention upon Judaism and Christianity, seeing the reconciliation of these Western religions as the necessary prelude to a harmonious relationship between the religions of the world.

Harold uses the King James Authorized Version of The Holy Bible, and James Moffatt's new translation of The Bible. At no time did he mention The Apocryphal New Testament, but I do, calling upon the Gospel of Thomas as Jesus' childhood is discussed.

I might say here that although Harold's view of Jesus is anything but traditional, he followed the tradition of capitalizing pronouns referring to Jesus. He also did this in referring to each of the world's great religious figures. My preference is to use lower case for pronouns referring to Jesus and other such figures. I trust that this will not detract from the text, since when quoting Harold I follow his practice of capitalizing pronouns.

I would like to say also that there are sections where one "blanket" reference is given at the beginning, since so many quotations are made that to list them individually would prove distracting to the reader. There are other passages where no reference is given, because references would detract from the dramatic effect I hope to create. In these cases placement of the text indicates that the passage is drawn from *The Shining Stranger*, which in *The Palestinian Mystery Play* takes the role of *The Stranger*.

Questions and comments from the "audience" are enclosed in quotation marks to indicate dialogue, and the spacing indicates "who" is speaking. Having called attention to these liberties I have taken, I will return to Harold.

To Harold, depth and growth psychology, operating in complementary fashion with a philosophy as expansive and penetrating as Oliver Reiser's, will provide the framework within which scientific investigation and religious expression can proceed in harmony to lead man nearer to the truth of his own being and that of his universal environment. Harold's ideas of depth and growth psychology will be dealt with in another book, *The Inner Messiah*, to be published soon.

Cosmic Humanism by Oliver L. Reiser[7] was not published during Harold's lifetime. But knowing the work of both authors as well as I do, I feel confident that had Harold lived to read this book and Dr. Reiser's subsequent writings, he would have been as appreciative of Dr. Reiser's work as Dr. Reiser has been of his. I am grateful to Dr. Reiser for his Introduction and Summary. I am indebted to him also for the title, "The Palestinian Mystery Play," which he suggested that I write with a view to incorporating it as a chapter in his forthcoming *Magnetic Moments in Human History*. But the Play grew to book length in itself, and so it is being published separately.

In my contribution to *The Single Reality*, I have tried tentatively to unite the thought of Reiser and Harold, because each man's philosophy is Cosmic in dimension and to me many of their ideas are complementary. I would like to point out, however, that it is not necessary to accept Harold's philosophy as a prerequisite to subscribing to Cosmic Humanism, which is on the forefront of time and stands in its own right as a philosophy seeking new dimensions to accommodate the evolving consciousness of mankind.

I must also point out that Harold did not once use the word *humanism*. He may have refrained because the word is associated with atheism and "heartless" scientism, to which he, most certainly, did not subscribe. But today there are religious humanists who seek only to transcend outgrown theologies, as Harold did. And in Cosmic Humanism I see a modern translation of "God is love." I have associated Harold's work with religious humanism. But like Reiser's, it, too, stands in its own right as a philosophy that adds dimension to science and religion.

I am also deeply grateful to Dr. Robert M. L. Baker, Jr., for writing the Preface for the Physical Scientist and for the suggestions he has given me to improve my part of this book. To have a physicist of his reputation and qualifications lend support to Harold's work and mine is indeed heartening and gratifying.

And I would like to thank Dr. Beatrice Bruteau, to whom I am indebted for the word *Logon* used in Book II, and Mrs. Daniel Ziegler II, for the helpful suggestions they made and the work they did on the manuscript and proofs in the process of producing this book.

Harold cast his work into anonymity. He was committed to the concept that truth must and will make its own way in this world. If the unknown author's thought touches upon truth, it will elicit response.

There have been many guesses as to who Harold might be. None strikes us as being plausible. Many questions have been asked—but nothing that Gerald Heard, Michael Barrie, or I could reveal in the way of small details would throw any actual light upon the mystery. Therefore, we have determined to say no more than is said here.

There is another reason for our silence. We do not know who the author was, but anyone presenting himself as the author would have to know the many details we will not reveal. The story of our part in the publication of Harold's work is written and will be held in the files of Harold Institute. We believe in the integrity of the author, and in the sincerity of his desire to remain anonymous. We also believe that he is deceased. Our knowledge makes it impossible for anyone but the author to claim the work.

Who and what was Harold? This question must remain. The kind of person he was shows in his work. In a letter to me, Professor Aarne Siirala of Waterloo Lutheran Seminary wrote, "*The Shining Stranger* is really fascinating. The more I read it, the more I am convinced of its impact. The inner coherence of Harold's thoughts is really fantastic. There is something in the spirit and in the personality of the unknown writer which is exceptionally humble, pure and clear, something which touches the reader deeply. Behind the book must be an extraordinary and solid person."

In the opening pages of *The Shining Stranger*, Harold tells us only this, "The new answer to the mystery of Jesus offered in this study has not been received through mystic revelation. It has presented itself of its own accord as into one fold were gathered as many of Jesus' words and as much of fact and philosophy as the limited mental capacity of one man could assimilate and express in a limited number of words. Many of these words are quoted. . . ." His book is dedicated to those he quotes.

The only statement Harold made about his scientific work was appended as an epilogue to "On the Nature of Universal Cross-Action" when it was first printed. It seems fitting now to use his statement in this Prologue, so that the reader may know in the beginning all there is to be known about the anonymous author. His statement is as follows:

The author of the hypothesis, "On the Nature of Universal Cross-Action," while studying the life and work of James Clerk-Maxwell, became intrigued by Maxwell's preoccupation with the New Testament and his efforts to interpret it. Suddenly, he felt that the bond between the great scientist and the Nazarene might be meaningful in a way not generally recognized, for both men had attempted to reveal the nature of *light*, and Clerk-Maxwell's brilliant intuitions might have stemmed, unbeknownst to him, from his mental immersion in the words and drama of Jesus.

Thus, there began a search of the Gospels from which Clerk-Maxwell drew his inspiration—indirectly, no doubt—and a search of the Old Testament, upon which Jesus drew heavily, to see if there could be found simple principles from which a theory of light might be drawn. The author did and did not find what he was looking for. The principles were there, as unobtrusive as electrons hidden in space, but from them a new and different theory—complementary, not contradictory—must be constructed.

In a climate so inhospitable to religion, however, to present this work giving credit to Jesus, author of the principles upon which it rested, was to foredoom it. Would any scientist so much as read the work, in Jesus' name?

As this question was being pondered, another question arose. If the hypothesis to be drawn from Jesus' principles provides a new interpretation of many of the phenomena with which scientists contend, and does not contradict the data they have gathered, although it leads beyond current concepts, might not the rest of the "fruit" of this tree be good? A fresh look at the whole of Jesus' work might reveal other principles in other disciplines. Most important, one might find the principles upon which a new interpretation of His mission could rest, thereby restoring faith in His integrity and giving *new meaning* to His message.

The larger work was begun, and the conviction grew that the hypothesis, "On the Nature of Universal Cross-Action," could not be presented apart from Jesus, the author of its principles, and that it must be stated first in terms any interested layman or student could understand.

My effort has been to present both the scholarly book, *The Shining Stranger*, and Harold's scientific theories, to the layman.

And now, because "the play's the thing,"[8] let us get on with it.

7

The Premise

The beginning of the Palestinian mystery play is lost in the dawn of the day man was cast from the womb of nature into a state of consciousness unlike that of any other living thing. He comprehended *life*, and himself as a creator who must be identified with the Cosmic creative cause, which he named "God." God-consciousness, Cosmic-consciousness, indeed, Cosmic Humanism, began in the coming of mankind's self-consciousness.

Ever more sophisticated conceptions of God followed man's changing conceptions of himself and nature. These realizations were passed from generation to generation by words, spoken, then written. Each sacred writ tells essentially the same story of God/Man.

A new organization of energy, and therefore a new *evolutionary force*, entered to shape this planet's history with the advent of mankind, because in him word power, *a new type of energy*, was initiated. The effect of word power upon the inorganic and organic realms is unknown because this power involves a synthesis of measurable physical energy (sound waves) and the unmeasurable, perhaps unknowable, human energy that man calls mental.

The advent of word power marked a magnetic moment in planetary history that makes all others pale in comparison. In this moment a creature broke out of the vicious circle of the animal world in which every member is an offensive and/or defensive *biological weapon*. Man is not. The breakthrough came *after* man had relinquished claws and fighting canine teeth. Naked of weapon, without cloak, he stood upright upon the earth, let his gaze travel to the stars—and beyond—seeking his ancestral home. He sought also the meaning of his consciousness that lifted him from the ground of Cosmic dust, and then from "all fours," causing him to evolve into an expression of life that cannot be completely identified with other living forms and their evolution.

8

Although from the beginning man knew himself to be a part of nature, he knew that his species stands apart from nature because he is vested with God-consciousness and word power, and this would be true wherever "man" appears in the universe. He knew that God is all of nature, yet God must stand apart from nature in man's mind because God is the creative force, the reality, the mind of the Cosmos that expresses itself to the fullest only in humankind.

What we know of evolution reveals man's kindredship with all living creatures. Yet he remains a greater mystery than he was before the work of Darwin and others appeared upon the scene. Man's evolutionary path, his behavior, his physical differences, his emotional responses, the dizzying rate of change to which he adapts—and which he expresses in the development of his consciousness, in his work, in his art—shows him to be so different from anything else he has known that he cannot be explained as the culminating product emerging from the material environment of which he is, undoubtedly, also a product. When all that is different about humankind is posed against the undeniable facts of biological evolution in the natural world, can we say that man is a product of lower life forms, or must we say that he is *chalice and residual expression of the creative force, the reality, of which the Cosmos is made?*—a parallel development in the animal kingdom, destined from the beginning cell of his life to have dominion over it.

But he will not realize this *dominion* until he understands the meaning of the word, which is: *supreme authority*—and until he understands that the supreme authority in life is *love and understanding*. He will not gain dominion by attempting to "lord it over" nature and all other creatures, acting the arrogant master and despoiler. He will realize his dominion when he realizes the power and glory of knowledge and love and expresses goodwill toward man and nature.

In *The Palestinian Mystery Play*, this is the case we will present: nature is the *devolution* of Parent Cosmic Energy, physical and mental, which preserved unique power and glory in one expression of itself, vesting this power and glory in humankind, when it had spent itself of all but one measure of its absolute and original power. Creation is entrusted to the operation of perfect natural law, which eternally renews and restores to perfect balance and satisfying likeness all that is essential to life, insuring its evolvement into an optimum state of change and being.

The verdict is left to you—the jury of readers.

9

The Beginning

God-consciousness opened man's eyes to behold the world in the allegorical human being named Adam-Eve with whom the Palestinian mystery play begins. Mankind spoke. The Cosmos changed. What man said altered the pattern that Cosmic energy took on in response to this altogether new stimulus arising from Planet Earth. Devolution ceased. The evolution of human consciousness began.

Such magnetic moments may have occurred elsewhere in the universe before or after. But the stars themselves felt the impact of earth man's first, "Hello, your name is—what?" This sound rang with a resonance no other sound could have. It was the Cosmic Voice, given into individual, independent expression. The word-maker had been led through nature's channels. Faith in the incipient God-power within him had led him to disarm his body. His sense of kindredship with the light in the skies above had raised him from the ground to stand upright. Love for life, for himself and his kind, led him into and out of the jungle mind, made him long for something else—something better.

Mankind was a being so different from all he beheld that he felt a sense of exile from nature. How different is he? In these ways, and more:

He is the only creature that possesses the gift of speech which he can use, because he alone has a chin.

He is the only true biped.

He is the most "naked" of all creatures that roam the face of the earth.

He lives the longest period of any creature in the helplessness of infancy and childhood—making the greatest demand upon his parents throughout life.

He (male and female) expresses sexual desire year around—not periodically, as other creatures do.

He is generally left- or right-handed—"asymmetrical" as opposed to the symmetry generally expressed in nature, which is ambidextrous. He is the only creature with a true thumb, making of his hand the world's most marvelous tool.

He is the only creature that sheds real tears and laughs real laughter. He is the only creature that "plays" his life long.

He is not a biological weapon—all other creatures are to greater or lesser degree "physical weapons" for offense and/or defense by virtue of their bodies or behavior, or both.

He possesses the greatest brain on earth and has unmatched capacity to learn, to imagine, and to create.

So endowed with "difference" is man that he is both the most helpless and the most powerful creature on earth.

Grounded in fear, yet driven by courage—an alien who was yet perfectly at home in earth through which his body had evolved from one-cell creature onward—man's consciousness called out to and from his very being, "O God, I am—what?" The question has not yet been answered. But mankind has never ceased to ask it.

As the Palestinian mystery play moved on from Adam-Eve to other sets of characters, the sounding of one note repeated itself. Whenever man tried to answer the question of his being, the Cosmic Voice *within him* answered, "I, One, am the Lord, *your* God." At intervals, prophets speaking in the name of "I, the Lord, God," promise that One will come who will reveal the meaning of that recurring answer; and this One will reveal in his person the power, glory, grace of God, Cosmos. The coming of this One will mark the entrance of God-Incarnate into the affairs of man to take over their management and usher in the golden age, bringing perfect justice and harmony on earth. This One will be the *Messiah*. He will be born into the House of David. This and many other prophecies concerning the Coming One were spoken through the voices of the prophets of Israel.

Not only in Palestine, but throughout the earth, the promise of an Avatar, or a Messiah called by many names, to usher in the golden age and reveal to man the true nature of his being, came in answer to his question, "Who and what am I?" As civilizations rose and fell, as leaders strode across the stage and into the wings of time, this promise as answer took on many meanings. By whatever name this One was called, the word meant "Son of God, or Deity incarnate, bearer of Cosmic truth." That which began as an idea of *God involved in human life* became so objectified that God was set apart from man's own being. Mankind in all cultures awaited the advent of God/Man—Messiah. Through Him, and only through Him, could the human problem be resolved. Through Him, freedom and the salvation of man's degenerating society would come.

In Palestine, Israel in bondage to Rome awaited the Coming One, in their urgency looking to Him for deliverance. And in Rome, seers were foretelling the coming of a succession of gods, leading to the renovation of the world. At that time, mankind on Planet Earth awaited and sought supranatural intervention and the advent of One or a series of Messiahs to save the human race from *itself*.

Jesus of Nazareth Takes the Stage

Into this waiting age, in Palestine, crossroads of the civilized world, Jesus was born. Little is known of his childhood. If the apocryphal Gospel of Thomas can be believed, the boy had extraordinary psychic power and exercised it in a way that must have made him the terror of his companions, his family, his village.[9] But the Gospel of St. Luke also tells us that by the time Jesus was twelve years old the brilliance of his mind astounded the astute scholars of Judaism.[10]

The Gospel of Thomas reports that Jesus refused to learn his "letters." He would not allow his teachers to discuss the "beta" (two) until they could explain to his satisfaction the meaning of the "alpha" (one). *One* is the number upon which arithmetic (through which mathematics is given practical meaning) rests. *One* is the number upon which each individual, the whole of the universe, the concept of God, of reality, rests.

The meaning of *one*, the principle upon which it operates, appears in Thomas's Gospel to be the dominating thought in the mind of the boy Jesus. As he explains the "alpha" to his teacher, Jesus' word-picture calls up a vision of the principles of geometry, a vision of the propagation of light, expressed as only an artist can express such as this. Artist I. Rice Pereira says:

> Unity (one) can be grasped only from a synthesis of a manifold. . . . This constitutes a unity of the *two*: the *senses* and the *intellect*. . . . *A third principle* stands outside of the two—the horizontal plane of the senses and the vertical plane of the intellect. . . . The third principle stands outside in order to unify the whole.

And then she explains:

> When the horizontal and vertical planes come into a balanced relationship, the third principle—the illuminative principle—transverses the whole

13

content. Thus the fourth principle comes into "Being." *The fourth is the form-giving principle* by means of which a structure of Reality is made manifest on the world-plane. The fourth principle is "Being." It brings into Reality the Formal structure of the content of the Whole. It contains the cosmic reason.[11]

Now, listen to the boy Jesus, according to the Gospel of Thomas, as Zacchaeus, the teacher, tells him all the letters from "Alpha even to Omega, clearly, with much questioning":

> But Jesus looked upon Zacchaeus the teacher and saith unto him: Thou knowest not the Alpha according to its nature, how canst thou teach others the Beta? thou hypocrite, first, if thou knowest it, teach the Alpha, and then will we believe thee concerning the Beta. Then began he to confound the mouth of the teacher concerning the first letter, and he could not prevail to answer him. And in the hearing of many, the young child saith to Zacchaeus: Hear, O teacher, the ordinance of the first letter and pay heed to this, how that it hath [what follows is really unintelligible in this and in all the parallel texts; a literal version would run somewhat thus: how that it hath lines, and a middle mark, which thou seest, common to both, going apart; coming together, raised up on high, dancing (a corrupt word), of three signs, like in kind (a corrupt word), balanced, equal in measure] thou hast the rules of the Alpha.[12]

Words of a difficult and precocious child? Or of a born mathematical genius? "Lines and a middle mark common to both"—this can call up only the vision of the bisected diameter of the whole, the *cross encircled*. "Lines going apart, coming together, raised up on high, dancing"—was the child envisioning the opposing frequencies of a light-wave group? "Three signs, like in kind, balanced, equal in measure"—was he describing the equal charges of *positive* and *negative* energy that accompany each other in nature to produce the third sign, *neutral*, which brings balance, wholeness, unity, *one*? How near to truth is the "literal version" that Montague Rhodes James gives us! These words are not unintelligible in the twentieth century—they are an astounding, although poetic, description of reality, as scientists perceive it.

From birth, this strange and brilliant child, Jesus, had been thought by his parents, and no doubt an inner circle, to be the long-awaited Messiah. He was born to Mary, a virgin, and was adopted by Joseph of the House of David. By design or through force of circumstance, Mary and Joseph fulfilled prophecies concerning the Coming One. For example, they took the child into and out of Egypt. When Jesus was twelve years old, the curtain dropped, and it did not rise again on the Palestinian mystery play until he began his ministry at about thirty years of age.

Legend tells us that Joseph of Arimathea, Jesus' uncle, took the boy to Glastonbury in England. If we give credit to the Gospel of Thomas and its reports of Jesus' extraordinary demonstrations of psychic power in childhood, these exhibitions in addition to his refusal to learn from his teachers provide reason for Jesus to be taken away from his home. Tensions must have mounted as his strange power and behavior caused consternation. If Joseph took Jesus to Glastonbury, he took him into the heart of the ancient history of his day—perhaps into the history of lost Atlantis—and certainly into the midst of teachers who understood his unusual psychic powers and could develop them to the fullest.

In Glastonbury, Jesus may have learned of the many phenomena arising from expression of psychic energy and how to employ it, utilizing its range from minimum to maximum degree. Because he was possessed of such large measure of psychic power, he could have come to understand it as few have before or since. According to the legend, Jesus came as a boy, stayed long enough to build a church, and left.

There is much to indicate that Jesus spent at least a part of the lost years in the community of the Essenes. Much has been revealed in the Dead Sea Scrolls to show the beliefs and practices of this group. Their influence upon Jesus, however it came about, is evident in his teaching. The Essenes must have played a major role in shaping his thought. How long he tarried among them is an open question. Today, we can also see the image of the great religions of Asia, as well as the traditions of Judaism, indelibly imprinted upon the body of Jesus' doctrine. A few examples that do not purport to be conclusive, but present likenesses, are:

Hinduism, with its emphasis on truth's outworking through karma, which is described in Jesus' words that pertain to sowing and reaping and to the measure a person has meted out being meted out to him.

Buddhism, with its insistence that apart from oneself there is no light, no Buddha—and Jesus' words that turn man to seek the kingdom of God within himself.

Zen, with its emphasis upon the "here-now" of the "pure land" and the inward working that brings one to perfection through practice of the commonplace in humble joy—and Jesus' statements indicating that the reign of God is in the midst of man, and in the midst of society, here now, working to insure that the humble in heart will inherit the earth, that the pure in heart will know God.

Taoism, with its dedication to nature, its worship in natural surroundings—and Jesus' like pattern, teaching by the seashore, turning men to consider the lilies of the field, the sparrows.

Space does not permit giving examples of the likenesses between the Chinese religions and Jesus' teaching, other than to say that the situations of change are held to be primary in life in the *I Ching*[13]—and this precept is echoed in Jesus' words that indicate all things are made anew.

Nor does space permit a discussion of the likenesses between Jesus' teachings and those of the Greek philosophers. But in the Gospels there are indications that Jesus was an educated man.

Here, the curtain must rise on that brief moment in time when Jesus played the starring role in the Palestinian mystery play. The strange child, grown into an even stranger man, described by Ernest Renan as the summit of human greatness,[14] the strongest individual force ever to come upon the earth, takes the stage.

This was a magnetic moment in the history of humankind. The words Jesus spoke reverberate today. They do not resonate with the theology that has been preached in his name. But they resonate with nature's voice ever more strongly as man begins to understand what the universal energy is "saying" as it speaks through him and through every manifestation in the Cosmos, from elementary particle to distant quasar. Everything seems to be "dancing lines" of energy expressing in wavelike motion.

The scene opens as John the Baptist, also strongly influenced by the Essene community, baptized Jesus. Then Jesus suffered the "temptation" in the wilderness, described as Satan's prompting him to use his power to rule the world. *This was what large numbers of people expected Messiah to do, thereby bringing on the Golden Age.* Jesus refused to respond to the tempting.

The ministry of the man of Nazareth then begins. As Jesus made his way through Palestine, he invited twelve men to work with him. Each responded almost spontaneously. There was a disciple known only as the "beloved." Today, he is called John. Gospel records say that the others were not a part of the learned world of Judaism. Jesus taught them in private, entrusting to them explanations of his meaning that could not be preached to the crowds that began to follow him. These disciples shared with Jesus a number of strange experiences—visionary, miraculous but elusive in nature.

Jesus taught the crowds also, using the words that are gathered in the

Sermon on the Mount—honesty, charity, love of neighbor is its theme. And he brought about many healings. As he came to the attention of the Judaic authorities, they questioned him closely. He challenged many of time's accretions to Mosaic Law, but he upheld the Ten Commandments, and spoke with an authority that astonished the people. He exhibited wisdom so profound that his questioners were unable to contend with him. He became *the personification of the "being question"*—Who and what am I?

From this scene onward, the Palestinian mystery play revolves around the question, "Who and what was Jesus?" Was he the long-awaited Judaic Messiah who for some reason refused to fulfill the role as he was expected to fulfill it—and was in turn refused by Judaism? Was Jesus, as Christianity came to assert, nothing less than God incarnate, playing the role of man, His creature—tasting the bitterest cup He could drink in order to bring Himself to forgive man's sin? Or was Jesus a man so deluded that he believed God, Cosmic Cause, had delivered into his hands all of humanity to judge and sentence to life or death, to heaven or hell, because he would make restitution for their sins by dying on the Cross? Or are none of these interpretations correct, so that the real mission and meaning of Jesus is not as yet understood?

As Jesus leaves the stage, the mystery that will dominate the next scene is set. He is thought to have died on the Cross—and he was buried in a tomb from which his body had disappeared on the morning of the third day. His followers insisted that he had then reappeared to them for a time, telling them again that *Son of man*, the title by which he called himself, would come back within the lifetime of the "beloved disciple." He had told his interrogators that they would *all* see the *Son of man* descending in glory upon the clouds of heaven. He had instructed his disciples to go forth and preach his gospel to the world; he had said that his Church was to be built upon the disciple Peter, "the rock." The Resurrection drama lasted forty days as the curtain slowly fell on fading scenes of Jesus' life on earth.

St. Paul Steps into the Starring Role

As the curtain rises on the "Acts" of Jesus' small band of followers, the Apostle Paul shares and then begins to dominate in the establishment of early Christian doctrine. It is a time of waiting for Jesus' return.

As the years passed and he failed to reappear, the *mainstay* of this new religion—indeed, the only ground it had or has to stand upon—appeared. The Gospels. The mystery of how, when, by whom they were written has not yet been resolved. But they "spoke again" with the authority, the profundity, the simplicity of Jesus. Because of them, Christianity could live on after the original band was gone.

It is hard to imagine a more improbable happening than Christianity's survival. The irrational and paradoxical turns the religion took during the course of its evolution match the irrational and paradoxical turns man took in his evolutionary journey. Christianity, as the world has known it, is based upon St. Paul's interpretation of the man he had never met; but Jesus' words evoked in him such resounding echoes of truth that his faith only grew stronger as time passed and the promise of the return of Son of man failed to materialize. The healing ministry of the disciples waned, Jesus did not come back, but the Christian community only grew stronger, despite persecution by the Jewish hierarchy and the later persecution by the Romans. Its greatest growth took place long after time had made it impossible for Son of man to return as promised during the lifetime of Jesus' contemporaries. The pivotal point upon which Christianity began was utterly shattered. Yet, the growth of the religion became synonymous with the growth of Western civilization.

As the structure of Christian theology was elaborated, the Church was built not upon the doctrine of Peter, "the rock," as given in the Gospels, but upon the doctrine of Paul—the man that Saul of Tarsus became after the blinding brilliance of Jesus overcame him on the road to Damas-

18

cus. Christianity is not the Religion of Jesus. It is the Religion of Paul, who drew his ethic of love from Jesus, the ethic the Church fails all too often to practice.

More than a computer would be needed to calculate the good versus the evil done in the name of Jesus by Pauline Christianity. This must be measured against the good versus the evil done by mankind to mankind before Jesus or Paul appeared on the scene. This must be measured against the projection of what type of society would have evolved had Jesus and Paul not undertaken their missions from which Christianity was derived.

The more powerful the Christian Church became, the more foreign it became to Jesus' teaching and to Paul's—the less it practiced what they preached. At the same time, around and within it such an edifice of magnificent ritual, sublime art, music, architecture, and literature was built that:

> I, still drawn to the faith of my youth
> Loving its beauty while doubting its truth,
> Wonder if beauty is not truer than truth.[15]

Strange, because for centuries the depravity of man was the Christian theme. This depravity was exemplified most surely in the treatment the Church accorded those who challenged its power—and, once power had turned the table, in the unconscionable persecution of the Jews that culminated in Nazism's brief triumph, which sickened the world. Not until 1968 were the Jewish people living today "exonerated" of guilt for the Crucifixion of Jesus. Those who have stood in the shoes of the "big fisherman" seem to have forgotten that Peter thrice denied knowing Jesus and that there is nothing in the Gospels or in the Epistles of Peter or Paul that calls for the subtle or overt destruction of the Jews.

Around the planet, Christianity spread its message: Jesus was the only incarnation of God this world has known. Salvation is possible only through acknowledging him as Saviour. He will return and this will mark the end of the world, the beginning of heaven and hell, between which mankind will be divided as Jesus judges each person who has or will ever live. Not even theologians will talk about the "meat" of the Christian message today—but there it is. It is incredible that intelligent people could have spent their lives defending and elaborating this theology. But they did.

Paradoxically, through the efforts of the clergy, who were honest and ardent truth seekers in every sense of the word, *the base of education was broadened* until this became a major function of the Christian

Church in all of its denominations and remains the shining light of its accomplishment today. Galileo, Copernicus, Kepler, Newton, and others too numerous to name worked out the problems of Christian theology that were posed by their findings as carefully as they worked out the mathematics of their discoveries.

Did these people, and millions of other human beings through the centuries who must be counted as intelligent, really believe in Christian theology? Or did they pay lip service only, as they nevertheless *responded to the Christian symbols that evoked action below the conscious level because these symbols correspond with psychic and natural truth* even though the theology of Christianity taken literally does not?

Ignoring the irrational, the unbelievable, the unintelligible, the great majority of the Western world must have practiced a "wordless" faith in God and man, in the Cosmos itself, calling themselves Christians because the symbols and rituals of the Church evoked a certainty within them, and the words of the Nazarene that filtered through the trappings struck the chord of resounding truth.

Christianity must coat its "theological pills" with the ethic of honesty and love—the practice of which was demanded by both Paul and Jesus. The difference between the doctrines of these two men is not one of ethics. It is much deeper seated. It is a question of the *psychology of man*—the answer to the question, "Who and what am I?"

> Paul answered, "You are not your own, you were bought for a price." By Jesus.[16]
> Jesus answered, "Ye are the salt of the earth, ye are the light of the world . . ." and even the least of you are brother-beings to me, the *same* that I profess myself to be, the Son of God, the Father. Scripture cannot be broken, "I said, Ye are gods . . ."—"Ye shall know the truth, and the truth shall make ye free."[17]

How could two answers be more contradictory? Traditionally, Christianity has spoken only out of the Pauline side of its mouth when it answers the being question. But Jesus has a spokesman of his own.

The Bible Begins Prompting the Actors

With the advent of the printing press, the Bible became available in the Christian world. This did not happen until the contents of it had been fixed for so many centuries that any tampering with it then or now could be only ridiculous. For the first time since Jesus had the starring role, *multitudes of people could come into direct contact with him through the Gospels.* This "second coming," however, bid fair to herald the "end of the world" for Christianity.

No sooner had the *words of Jesus* in the Holy Writ begun prompting the actors in the Palestinian mystery play than Christianity began to come apart at the seams. That is, theology did. People began interpreting the "word" for themselves. New denominations of Christianity arose. There were many alterations to the orthodox theme. Even so, by the time the curtain was raised on the midnineteenth-century scene, the audience simply "filed out" mentally whenever a theologian rose to speak his piece. Soon they were leaving literally, and in droves by the time the mid-twentieth-century began its act.

Belief in the orthodox doctrine of the Christian churches failed so rapidly that even the "believers" were unaware that they no longer really accepted the dogma. But the stage was still full of the cast that played the role of followers. They clung to their parts, even after heaven knows how many theologians themselves ceased to believe in the Apostles' Creed, which they nevertheless dutifully recited.

From the nineteenth century onward, Christian theology became, in large part, an apology for what it had been—and a suitable whipping boy was found. The whipping boy was none other than the Holy Bible itself—especially the four Gospels. Scholars set out to show that the Gospels and the strange story they told—replete with accounts of miracles that science scoffed at—were not altogether true. Indeed, they were just about altogether false. Words such as *kerygma,* which refers to the content of the "early Christian message," were developed to give the appearance of technical competence and authority to the process of "Jesus Research" and "Form Criticism." If you do not believe that this is all that Christian scholars and theologians will talk about or teach today, try them and see for yourself.

Any passage that was found to be embarrassing to Christianity could be "read out of the record" on the ground of "misguided" kerygma, or it was found to be spurious for some other reason, or it was an interpolation of a dissenting group, or it was found to be at odds with the prevailing attitudes and practices of the day, or the passage was omitted in the most reliable Gospel, or it was contradicted in another. The Gospel of St. John came under such heavy attack that some scholars rose to defend it—scholarly works repudiated each other. Some researchers took refuge in the Old Testament legends, coming to their defense, showing that they are based upon historical fact. Others saw them as a "biased" history of the Israelites. In sum, a case was made for and against the authenticity and reliability of every part of the Bible, each of the Gospels, and every account of Jesus' works and words.

As we observe the twentieth-century scene, it is played against a backdrop of the shreds and tatters of the Gospels. Jesus is bypassed—his meaning is a question that is brushed under the rug. No one will discuss it. Some theologians flog the dead horse of their orthodox doctrine as though it can be brought to life if they abuse and disclaim it sufficiently. Others act as though belief in it can be renewed and sustained if they ignore it and devote themselves to belated good works on the social scene, involving Christianity so deeply in the problems of the day that the world will forget all that is implicit in its creed.

The simple fact of the matter is that *Jesus and the Gospels are indivisible.* There is no other record of him. In disclaiming the truth of this record, Christians themselves have sawed off the limb upon which they must sit; they have undermined the only ground upon which they can stand; they have made suspect *their only reason for being.*

No amount of research will erase the compelling fact that the four Gospels cannot be rewritten; they will confront Christianity as long as it exists. The story of the man who took the stage so many centuries ago cannot be retold, and it cannot be untold. When it is told, it evokes a response that cannot be explained in rational terms. It goes too deep. It stirs something in the depths of man that he is just now beginning to be aware of: an authority within himself that *matches the certainty* with which the Palestinian asserted himself to be uniquely the Son of the Creator of the Cosmos, of the universal energy that expresses throughout, but expresses itself to the fullest only in the mind of man.

The integrity of Jesus depends upon the integrity of the Gospels. There is no Jesus other than the Jesus of this record, and certainly there is no reason for Christianity to continue to exist if the sacred writ it is founded upon is invalid. It cannot survive on a diet of "Form Criticism" and "Jesus Research." Nor can it survive if it must depend upon the notion that "God on high" somehow pushed the pen of the men who wrote the Bible so that it was supranaturally created. Christianity must pin its hopes upon finding answers other than these as to how the miracle that the Bible is, came to be wrought. And miracle the Bible continues to be. Whatever is said about it, it continues to prompt men to action and to higher levels of consciousness. Is it not a living edition of Homo sapiens himself?

Miracle of the Twentieth Century—The Return of Palestine to the Children of Israel

The stage upon which the Palestinian mystery play takes place has many sets. The actors become audience for each other. As Christianity waxed, Judaism did not wane. It persisted, although driven from set to set, and sometimes underground to find a place to continue its part in the drama. In the twentieth century, no less a miracle than many reported in the Old Testament occurred when the governments of the Christian world brought their power to bear and returned Palestine to the Children of Israel.

The fact remains that if the Judaic interpretation of Jesus and his meaning—that he was not the Messiah, not God incarnate—is right, then the Christian interpretation of him is wrong, and vice versa. The beliefs of the Judaic and Christian communities remain in complete opposition, each a denial of the other. In view of this, there is no greater mystery than the return of the remnant of Israel to its homeland, its ancient prophecy that heralds the Golden Age fulfilled for it by the action of the Christian world.

But by the time the miracle of Palestine-regained occurred, Christian theology was so well watered that tolerance prevailed. And the Christian community *had been forced back into its antecedent Judaic belief*—there is one God who will someday reveal Himself to man. Christianity had become and continues to be more Judaic than Christian. The meaning of Jesus was the thorn in its side—still is.

As though this mystery play were not contrary enough, by the time Palestine was returned to the Jewish people, ancient prophecy fulfilled, the Jewish people, too, began to file out of the audience as their orthodox theologians spoke. Their age-old Messianic tradition bids fair to join Jesus, under the rug, where it is brushed. Few Jewish people will discuss it.

Judaic rituals are observed, lip service is paid. There remains, of course, the hard core of the committed, just as there is in Christendom. But among the educated, commitment wanes.

Meanwhile, on the Palestinian set itself, Islam contends with the miracle the Christian world wrought in returning Israel to the Holy Land and the ensuing displacement of the Arabic population. The Islamic community takes small comfort in the knowledge that Judaism is the mother lode from which this religion, as well as Christianity, was drawn.

Islam is an offshoot of a Christianity that had grown intolerable to some of its adherents centuries ago. They, nevertheless, revere Jesus as a prophet of the same God who made his *final and complete revelation* through the prophet Mohammed. Islam reads its lines from the Koran.

Israel has done a miraculous job in Palestine, both in turning it from desert to garden spot and in protecting its position there. The surrounding Islamic countries have not and no doubt cannot come to terms with the situation until their displaced peoples are reestablished and their own situations are somehow made more viable. But beneath and overhanging the apparent causes, economic and otherwise, that lead to unceasing strife, are the reverberations of a holy war. So deep are the scars, so fresh are the wounds, that it may well be that only a true reconciliation between the contending religions can pave the way for peace on the social scene.

The world, however, is no longer listening to the religionists fretting in the wings. Some time ago, as among educated people the world over belief in the orthodox doctrines of *every* religion began to wither, Science stepped into the starring role.

Science Upstages Religion

THREE SONS OF ISRAEL—MARX, FREUD, EINSTEIN— SPEAK THEIR PIECES

Science is involved in the Palestinian mystery play because much in the development of Science was brought about by people whose Judaic and Christian backgrounds often played a part in the shaping of their thought and scientific research.

By the nineteenth century, a *community of belief* such as the world had never before known began to develop in Science—belief in its methods, findings, theories. Scientists were bound in fellowship more real than any other that mankind has experienced. Community of belief allows Science to speak with authority. But until recent decades what Science said was as far from the true nature of energy and the universe as religions were far from the true nature of God, and as nineteenth-century capitalism was far from the practice of an ethical economy.

What capitalist could look back into the practices of early industrialism and wish to perpetuate the abuses that were the accepted norm of Marx's day? Who could tolerate nineteenth-century economic practices or theological demands? Karl Marx repudiated Religion and addressed himself to correcting economic injustice. He became the "high priest of atheism," and declared himself the infallible prophet of history.

Is a man an atheist when he rejects the theology of the nineteenth century—Judaic or Christian? Shortly before his death Marx said, "I am not a Marxist."[18]

Perhaps Marx's deepest meaning was, "I am not an atheist." He must have come to understand that each person comes in the end to believe in something, however hard he tries to sift his existence into "nothing." And "nothing" is itself another name for God, if "nothing" is what a man believes in. At the end, Marx came to grips with human nature—

26

economic and religious. Hence, he repudiated his "infallible" doctrine before he died.

God is a condition of man's being—the condition of his necessity *to believe* as a prerequisite to sanity and action. When belief in one set of propositions fails, belief in another must take its place. Karl Marx became the Messiah, and Marxism became a religion that took the place of declining orthodoxies for many people the world over. These actors read their lines from the *Manifesto*. And this religion, too, is akin to Christianity (therefore to Judaism), in that as Khrushchev put it, "We have taken many of the precepts of Jesus."[19]

Marxism and communism are not synonymous. The first is a "religion." The second is an economic and political system that is simply a monolithic corporation and a paternalistic, completely authoritarian government engineered by Lenin.

As Marxism waxed and orthodox religions waned, our mystery play took another paradoxical turn. *Marxism saved the life of the system it had set out to destroy*. Marxism became the catalyst which so speeded the evolution of industrialism into modern capitalism with its more ethical practices that the economy of the Western world escaped the inevitable doom that its nineteenth-century portrait portended. Capitalism lived to become the most viable system on the economic scene, because it rapidly opened itself to the most beneficial of the socialistic practices. Its evolution in this regard continues. The essential principles of capitalism are contained within the evolutionary process, however, so that incentive is sustained.

Again, paradoxically, as communism waxed, Marxism, as a religion, waned. It became apparent within a few decades that Marxism could never be a "substitute religion" which would satisfy men's souls or forever insure that their material needs would be met. By the midtwentieth century, in order for communism to sustain itself, it had to begin to admit into its operation the capitalistic practice that human nature demands—the profit incentive. Slowly, very slowly, communism begins to evolve.

It would take more than a computer to calculate the good and the evil done in the name of Marx. Whatever the score, as a religion, Marxism declined as rapidly as it arose, sharing the fate of traditional religions. And, paradoxically, Science, which had appeared to be the infallible "religion," found itself in the same boat.

Judaism lives in a state of crisis. In the twentieth century, Christianity found itself in acute crisis. Then the Religion of Science—belief in Science as savior, hope of the world, bearer of the golden age—found itself in a state of crisis. Science had proliferated into more sects and denominations than religions could claim. Each had become so exclusive that *communication* in the "grand fellowship" began to falter and then to fail. Laymen had long since given up attempts to hold "dialogues" with the scientific world, which is now a veritable Tower of Babel; and the "confounding" of its tongues continues as ever more obscure words are coined to convey what seems to be a convoy of answers, but turns out to be a convoy of questions.

Onto the scientific set exact and inexact sciences had crowded. Sigmund Freud had seen this place as the "promised land" for psychology. But Freudian psychology, brought to stand examination in the light that psychology itself had cast upon the dark inner world of man, was found to be "sicker" than the sick religions it had tried to displace. Psychology was upon us—more threatening and demanding and degrading than "Jehovah" in his worst fit of temper or pique. And the cry went up, "O God, save us, but don't shut up sex in Pandora's box again."

Then a funny thing happened. Physics woke up one night and found Psychology in its bed. Carl Jung and Wolfgang Pauli turned Physics and Psychology to face the microscopic and macroscopic problems of inner space and outer space as parallel problems, which could well have parallel answers, laws, processes.[20] The idea was stated, but never precised. Physics and Psychology remain strange bedfellows, puritanical in their approach to each other, the union unconsummated.

But more than a cacophony of disciplines, each whirling in a *cul de sac* of its own making (as were the religious sects of the world), toppled the high and mighty structure outgrown from nineteenth-century Science. Another son of Israel, Albert Einstein, who had shifted his attention from Judaism to exploring the mysteries of nature, spoke up. His concepts and a resulting equation, simple and profound, shook the stars. The universe felt the impact of $E = mc^2$.

How far into space have the energy patterns spread that were born of that convulsive moment when Enrico Fermi could say that this equation stated workable truth? From this moment onward, Science became a more "absolute terror" than God had ever been. For Science had brought down upon our heads the "day of judgment"—*the day when judgment must take over from power* to solve the problems of the world. This was a magnetic moment in the history of man. An understatement. There are no words to describe the import of this moment. It may mark the beginning of our utter destruction. Or it may have been a signal to the Cosmos,

"Earth is ready to peck out of its shell. Our embryonic and fetal days are over. Our soma cells have taken their places in organs, tissue, muscle, blood, limbs, and brains—in a marvelous number of organizations. Taken together, mankind is a body of consciousness, coming into Cosmic awareness, ready to explore the mansions of this solar system—even others."

The audience is not listening.

For a hundred years, the drums of the Religion of Science have been rolling one note that accompanies every trill of discovery: *Nihilism*. Here is its pitch: Nature's supreme law, the second law of thermodynamics, which has been found to govern every expression of energy— and to be involved even in the expression of the *word*, in communication —says that the universe is dying a heat-death. Every celestial body in the system is dying. The organization of energy which provides the fuel that is consumed to supply the warmth that life needs is being constantly disorganized with subsequent loss of temperature—in every move made, or even if a system is left to itself—and there is no evidence in the purely physical sense that it is being reorganized.

Let us hasten to say that not all scientists hold this view. In fact, more and more of them are now refusing it. But for a long time it held sway. This is the doctrine of an ungodly materialism wherein it is presumed that everything in creation feeds like a parasite upon the stuff of its Cosmic host until the host's energy is consumed and both go down to destruction.

Relatively speaking, not a handful of people on this planet have any idea of what nature's supreme law is or how it works—not even the most highly educated people. But it is the scientists' interpretation of this law that is grinding like the salt mill at the bottom of the ocean of modern knowledge, flavoring the whole of it so that it is no longer potable for man's soul. Artists may not be aware of this law, but they are aware of the despair that flavors life; and they are aware of the repudiation by the young not only of today's value system, but their repudiation of the idea that there can be a valid value system if life, evolution, and the universe are meaningless and purely materialistic.

To the degree that man *believes he is a thing*, product of blind and purposeless nature that *is moving toward senseless oblivion*, be assured that *he will act* according to this belief. Life is bereft of a motivating *principle*.

Space age in a dying universe? So what? An unmotivated audience amuses itself. And "happenings," hapless, light the dark theater like fireflies on a warm June night. The bright promises of Science and technology fall on deaf ears. What *value* can there be in such a system, even if it will take billions of years before its witless course is run? If this is actually the condition of the universe, it holds forth no reason, no promise, to man.

The good and the evil done in the name of Science are difficult to measure. Against its triumphs, we must pose our polluted environment, our scarred and blighted landscape, our souls sucked dry of purpose in being. On the other hand, Science has unquestionably been a blessed benefactor to life, a purifying discipline that has rid us and Religion of many a false and foolish notion. No doubt, in time technology will bring great abundance—affluence everywhere on this planet. This is not enough. Across time come the words of the mysterious Nazarene, "a man's life consisteth not in the abundance of things which he possesseth"—man does not live by bread alone, the body is more than raiment.[21]

The Religion of Science offers no food for the soul. A wave of fear sweeps over the audience as they see so many of the brightest, most dedicated young people of this decade say to Science and to the traditional religions, now making feeble overtures to each other, "A plague on both your houses."

And the Religion of Science is in the same fix as the rest of the religions. No one does much more than pay lip service to the doctrine of *Nihilism* and blind materialism. There is a certainty in man which prohibits faith in "nothing." Science itself numbers among its members countless devoutly religious men, in that they cling to their faith in the Cosmos, God; as they observe its marvelous working and order, the similarity of its underlying patterns of operation, they express or feel confidence in its sanity. Like the theologians, they can neither fully accept nor fully reject their own doctrines. And they share in another dilemma.

Science is as fixed in Messianic expectation as ever Judaism and Christianity were. You do not believe it? Consider that Messiah by any name or definition is a *perfect entity*, superior to the limitations and transitoriness of man and nature—therefore, mystical and not altogether explicable. Now, listen to Gerald Holton speaking of Science's seeking such an entity:

> This entity, superior to all limitations and even above man's thought, is easily recognizable in scientific thought, from the beginning to this day, as the conception—a haunting and apparently irresistible one despite all evidence to the contrary—of the final, single, perfect object of knowledge to which the current state of science is widely thought to lead us, more or less asymptotically, but continually and inexorably. Like the exemplification of this conception outside science—in the Supreme Being,

or the millennial utopia—the final state of science is one that is generally agreed cannot be defined with any degree of precision by means of concepts or the use of ordinary language. That would be incompatible with its perfection. It is seen as a conception far beyond those arising directly from an examination of the empirical world. Occasionally a scientist rashly dares to put this dream into words, and then it is likely to emerge that the best he can say is that the goal has already been achieved.[22]

You see? Science, too, must deal with the Messianic claims of its early adherents, and with its persisting Messianic expectation.

Paradox enters the picture. *As the Messianic complex of all religions withers*—and all of them are infected with it to some degree, including the Religion of Marxism and its opponent, the Religion of Democracy—*the Messianic complex of Science blossoms*. This is strange because it was the Messianic-mindedness of traditional religions that led Science to distrust them—their various assertions that (1) the "perfect entity" could be produced only within the vessel of their particular group, (2) the "perfect entity" had been produced by a particular group, (3) this "Messianic dream" was possible of realization.

Science decries the Messianic complex that has haunted the history of mankind's religious expression. "Give us the facts," Science says, "and we will construct valid theories that warrant belief." Well, then, here are the facts: Science is suffering a serious if not critical case of Messianic pretension and delusion. What does Science make of that?

It appears to us that the Messianic complex is a condition common to mankind and every individual is likely to suffer it sooner or later to some degree because it involves the will to power, and the notion that truth can be had by the exertion of the intellect, to the exclusion of intuitive gleanings or certainties based upon feelings and vice versa.

Perhaps this continuously shifting spectrum in which Messianic delusion is bandied between men of intellectual bent and men of intuitive bent—between Science and Religion—can be understood better if we blow up the picture to Cosmic proportions. We will use one of Rudolf Thiel's "Modern Fables of the Stars." He describes a certain pair of stars as cannibals. Here is his description of them:

> The partners whirl around one another in four hours. As a result, both are distorted; they form a kind of double egg, with ends almost touching. The smaller of the two stars has emitted a gaseous appendage that is wrapped around its big partner. But horrible to relate, the big one is sucking the substance out of the little one, as a spider might a fly. The

end, however, will not be fatal, said astronomer Paul Guthnick. Soon
the smaller star's turn will come, he maintains, and it will feed on its
partner for a few years, until the big one is only a skeleton of its former
self. Then the whole procedure will begin over again.[23]

This is a pretty gruesome story—but, then, it depends upon how you
look at it. It would make no difference whether we liken the big star or
the little star to Religion or Science. Each takes its turn of waxing fat and
waning lean—of glutting itself with will to power and claim to all truth,
or claim to be the vehicle that has or can absorb and radiate all truth. But
as one of them attempts to draw all substance from the other and leave it
but an empty shell, it partakes on the one hand of the delusion that
bloated and on the other hand of the pretension that collapsed the structure into a body composed of a good deal of degenerate matter.

But, let us look at the fable in another way. It would make no difference whether we called the big star or the little star the intellect versus
the intuition. The drama would say that there are times when truth can
express itself best in the house of intellect, times when it can express itself
best in the house of intuition—but the essential thing is that the cyclic
cross-action does not destroy *either house*, it simply allows for resting
the forces of each. Since this cycle repeats itself so often, it must be seen
as a continuous play between the two forces. The scene begins to look
now like the most "Cosmic kiss" the Cosmic Imagination could dream up
—no doubt an expression of lust of Cosmic proportions. And it is not
to be expected that Science and Religion would be comfortable in such
a passionate embrace. But it would be in line with the facts of the case if
Science and Religion could see themselves as a "double egg" germinating
planetary consciousness and Cosmic awareness in mankind.

Scientists are aware that, in concert with observation, *discovery* depends
upon and has come from the *intuitive* promptings and inexplicable flashes
of insight, quantum jumps in understanding, that mark the history of
mathematics and research in every field. The creative, innovative capacity in man rests upon his intuition, not logic. But intellect and reasoning power must be called upon to precise the ideas that intuition hands
to consciousness. They must be stated in workable and transmissible
terms, and they must be oriented within the body of human knowledge.
The ability of a trained and disciplined mind to receive the ideas *and* to
precise them leads to the expression of genius in Science that has sent it
soaring at rocket speed. With precious few exceptions, men of genius
in Science have been deeply, mystically, religious—some orthodox, some

unorthodox. But Science as a body abhors mysticism. It should. Because mysticism as such, mysticism that repudiates intellectual probing and refuses to deal with reason, is not only as sterile as intellectualism that refuses to consider psychic phenomena seriously, but it is apt to be a shady business.

Mysticism does not begin this way, but bereft of the correcting discipline that intellect and reason provide, it degenerates—sometimes into petty swindling, sometimes into a menacing expression of the will to power over others, sometimes into a misguided attempt at self-control, sometimes into a futile effort to escape reality.

When men of intellect, men grounded in reasoning power and logic, refuse to deal with psychic phenomena, a "black market" that deals in intuition appears. Investigation of the "occult" moves underground. Mankind will not have done with the subject. The entertainment industry is quick to capitalize upon the public's fascination. Morsels of fact are elaborated into such farce insofar as truth is concerned that Science is given still another reason to turn its back on the subject of psychic phenomena.

Mankind's fascination continues because intuition and individual experience insist that there is a power that may be projected outward and inward, a power that cannot be explained in physical, sensory terms. And there is a certainty in man that insists that death is not the end of the individual's life.

Today's "occult dramas" are usually set in a pseudoscientific scene. The public forgets that the type of science fiction that keeps "coming true" involves achievement in the realms of physics and chemistry—hard and exact sciences. The directors of the drama do not forget this. Therefore, the modern witches' brew is an array of instruments—tubes, lights, and dials. And there is a morsel of truth in the suggestion that "hard scientists" are investigating psychic phenomena "by night" as they practice their professions "by day" because the prejudicial attitude of the scientific community necessitates their keeping the two areas of research separate if they are to continue to operate within the Establishment.

There are other scientifically trained people, however, who are openly devoting their lives to research in psychic phenomena because they realize that this is the great frontier to be explored, using the methodology of Science insofar as is possible. They realize that until Science comes to grips with the many states of human consciousness, scientists are not dealing with the most compelling question that faces them.

There is no denying the evidence of inexplicable psychic and physical phenomena occurring as a result of hypnosis. But hypnotism, even the word, is shunned by most. We need but one movie (viewed by millions on TV) which solves its mystery by saying that the criminal or victim was hypnotized, to set research in this most important field back another year or two. There is good reason, no doubt, for the public to be wary. This simply emphasizes the need for Science to do full-scale research.

To be in a state of hypnosis is simply to be in a state of trance, which varies in degree from momentary unawareness to deathlike oblivion. It is likely that all states of consciousness are states of trance, because we are seldom if ever completely aware of every stimulus impinging upon us. In the hypnotic state, suggestion is the tool. There are as many degrees of response to suggestion as there are states of trance. All stimuli "suggest" something.

Any tool can be used constructively or destructively. Most tools can be turned into weapons, but most tools serve life well. One of the most valuable tools in nature's chest is—or could be—hypnosis. Every human being should be trained to use this psychic power beneficially for self and others, if called upon. And every human being should be taught how to defend against its misuse. Knowledge of the dynamics of hypnosis and its possibilities should be made common. Only when knowledge is *not* common can it be dangerous. The closely guarded secrets of what we call hypnosis are very probably at the root of all the "mysteries" and "strange cults." Releasing this strange power in the mind of man is a goal that could not, and cannot, be reached until and unless ethics keep apace.

Today, there is extraordinary interest on the part of the public in the occult, the metaphysical, the parapsychological. Such interest is likely to increase—leading to a discipline that may be called "paraphysics"—because scientific knowledge has led to such refinement of physical energy that research, in order to strike a new vein of knowledge, may well lead into areas that are paraphysical and metaphysical. Materialism has reached the end of its rope only to discover that it is still but a short way up the "mountain of mystery" that life and universal energy present. Knowledge has reached what may be called the "para-meta" plateau, and this is the *natural consequence of scientists' accomplishments*.

The questions have become "para-meta"—exploration of space, for example, demands extraterrestrial geography. And the scientific study of human consciousness demands that physics join with metaphysics to discover, for example, the effect of *sound* upon consciousness and flesh, the effect of consciousness upon the body, and the effect of word power, suggestion, upon mind and body because sound and mind are involved and therefore involve physics and metaphysics. Does the brain become a superconductor of Cosmic mental energy that recharges the mind when a person is in that blessed state of *trance* called meditation? Krishnamurti describes it beautifully:

> Meditation is a never-ending movement. You can never say that you are meditating or set aside a period for meditation. It isn't at your command. Its benediction doesn't come to you because you lead a systematized life, or follow a particular routine and morality. It comes only when your heart is really open. Not opened by the key of thought, not made safe by the intellect. But when it is as open as the skies without a cloud, then it comes without your knowing, without your invitation. But you can never guard it, keep it, worship it. If you try, it will never come back again: do what you will, it will avoid you. Because in meditation, you are not important, you have no place in it, and the beauty of it is not you, but in itself. And to this you can add nothing. Don't look out of the window hoping to catch it unawares, or sit in a darkened room waiting for it: it comes only when you are not there at all, and its bliss has no continuity.[24]

We cannot call for a moment of meditation—it will not come. So, give attention, please!

Something has been happening on every set that crowds the stage. For a number of years, the wise men of the East have been returning, quietly bearing their gifts to the Western world.

The Light of Asia Is Again Shed
upon the Western Scene

Asiatic religions are marching in force across the Western scene, and throngs are going forth to greet them. Gurus are in demand. As the various Oriental doctrines are taught, those who have ears to hear, eyes to see, are beginning to understand that every great religion in the world speaks the same truth and presents itself as representation of the being-truth of man. The wisdom of Asia is feeding the starving soul of Western man. The advent of these religions has turned *The Palestinian Mystery Play* into "theater in the round." Religion is observed from its every point of view—its "sets" girdle the planet.

But as the Asiatic religions wax in the West, they wane in the East, where Science and technology are being imbibed as rapidly and happily as the wine of Eastern religions is being imbibed in our sphere. All over Asia, among the educated, faith in traditional religions with their prohibitions and restrictive customs is declining. Need we say that large numbers of the populace are paying dutiful lip service and are cherishing the beauty that is attendant upon the rituals and festivals? This is true. Loyalty remains—conviction does not.

Just as a mother cannot hold in bondage the healthy adult, so the old orthodoxies—be they of Religion, of Science, or political in nature—cannot hold in bondage a consciousness that has outgrown them. But we can see, now that the play is "theater in the round," that the *church* of every religion in the world plays the mother role for mankind. Through the ages, religions have borne the legends, symbols, and sacred writings that provide the material from which humanity freely fashions its own body of philosophy in secret. Churches meet the need of the "children" of this world. They feed the emotional hunger of man and cushion his irrationality with their own irrationality. More effectively than any other organ in society, the churches teach ethics and divert man from criminal

36

expression, allowing him to wear a hair shirt if he must or to love life and serve his fellowmen. Be this mother lode as full of frailty as the human mother, she is better than none. Man's churches must be supported.[25]

Man, the individual, returns to his "mother faith" for sustenance and comfort in times of tribulation and crisis. This regression into childlike faith sustains him. The person who has no grounding in a mother faith, be the faith pantheistic, deistic, theistic, is indeed in jeopardy when inner or outer threats beset him. Because for many, if not for all, *faith is the condition on which sanity itself rests* as time bears life's inevitable stress into the here-now state of being, whatever it is. And faith, whatever it is in, is all that man has to fall back, move forward, or mark time on.

Man has outgrown the orthodoxies of the past—even of recent decades —but he has not outgrown his need for Religion, his compulsion to act out whatever he believes, and in one way or another to support the doctrine that "mothered" him or his kind.

As the whole scene is viewed, the power of the word becomes evident. Centuries of preaching the brotherhood of man are bearing fruit in a society that demands that this doctrine be practiced in spirit and in truth. True brotherhood goes far beyond according equal dignity to each sex, age, and race. It demands harmony between the religions, between the sciences and religions, between the governments of man.

A true community of belief that will lead to unified purpose and constructive action on every front is the need of this age. Community of belief neither requires nor permits the sacrifice of individuality. Each discipline, faith, race, and sex is required only to express in its own way the fundamental principles that apply to all, just as scientists the world over utilize the same mathematical principles.

There can be no real community of belief until there is a unifying concept as regards the nature of man and the Cosmos—a concept with which all the actors and the audience can identify. Today, each religion or ideology that has a place on the world stage tacitly repudiates all of the others because, despite their toleration, each is exclusive and each is awaiting, seeking, serving, or acting the part of its own version of Messiah that in the end tolerates no other version.

Everywhere, people are seeking the meaning that underlies the external structures—the meaning of Religion *and* Science in the history of man. Is not the propagation of Science as great a mystery as the propagation of Religion in the history of humankind? Mankind is seeking a faith of *Cosmic dimension.* And the *audience insists upon becoming a part of the play.*

The scene shifts. The stage is wherever the action is—in the pit, on

37

the balcony, in the boxes, or in any "cornered space" in this "theater in the round."

Now an unknown voice begins to speak through a book he left behind when the end of his life ended the Palestinian mystery play for him. Who or what this author was can never be known. Those who published his manuscript do not know his identity. His "script," *The Shining Stranger*, must speak for itself.

The title is taken from a line, "*truth* is often a shining stranger. . ."[26] —it refers to no person. The pen name of the author, Preston Harold, expresses in part what this author felt to be the truth of mankind—truth so beautifully spoken by Lord Byron in *Childe Harold's Pilgrimage*:

> . . . there is that within me which shall tire
> Torture and Time, and breathe when I expire;
> Something unearthly, which they deem not of.[27]

Preston Harold offers answers that the world has never heard before to the many questions raised by the Palestinian mystery play and its evolution into the "science fiction" of our day, which says God is dead and the Holy Ghost, the Cosmos, is dying.

Since audience participation is now the thing, let us hear in Act Two what *The Shining Stranger* has to say. We will ring down the curtain on Act One with Harold's premise:

> Stating a valid, rational, ethical, and soul-satisfying religious concept is the problem that confronts humankind with each enlargement of the boundaries of consciousness. Whatever else may appear on the surface to be engaging the efforts and attention of Homo sapiens, religion is the fundamental problem he deals with, for at base it concerns the problem of himself, the question of "Who and what am I?" . . . Such a religious concept must be psychologically based. Only then can it be universally valid.

This transition from theology to psychology, in understanding the meaning of Religion in man's history, can come simply as "each man takes a new view of his own religion."[28]

ACT TWO

The Shining Stranger Speaks

A New Answer to the Question of Jesus' Messiahship

Jesus appeared on the scene when the whole world was waiting for an external or supranatural force, personified in the person of a Messiah, to intervene in the affairs of man and accomplish for him all that he is potentially capable of accomplishing. History and the evolution of consciousness were marking time. Jesus *reversed* the force of Messianic expectation by assuming the role of Messiah and at the same time repudiating it. *The Shining Stranger* says:

> Jesus, Himself, so thoroughly undermined the prevailing Messianic concept, left the question of it and His relationship to it so entangled in contradiction, so twisted and bent in every direction, that the controversy He began could not be closed, the question could not be answered, the battle He started could not cease, until the last fragment of any Messianic image was gone and His own Messianic image, become in time a hated object of odium, had been pounded into dust.[29]

Therefore, Preston Harold concludes: *Jesus was not, and did not believe Himself to be, the long-awaited Judaic Messiah. His mission was to destroy the Messianic tradition of his day and supplant it with the idea of God indwelling every person, each expressed as God-son, Logos, Christ—or chalice of the life and unique power of universal parent being.* This is, indeed, a strong statement. But Harold develops a strong and solid basis for it, drawing upon Jesus' own words and actions. The case for this conclusion is presented in Chapter 2 of *The Shining Stranger*, and is elaborated in each succeeding chapter as the various aspects of Jesus' life and work are discussed. Each reader must draw his own conclusion as to the validity of this interpretation of Jesus' Messianic mission. To Harold, it is inescapable, because it rests upon Jesus' statements as given in the Gospels—not upon St. Paul's interpretation of the man he had never met. *The Stranger* says that Jesus counted on the stubborn integrity of his people to continue their refusal of him as Messiah, thereby keeping the question open until his actual meaning came to be understood. And this was his meaning: *Jesus saw that each person speaks of himself only in the name of God, which is "One, I." Speaking in this name, Jesus deliberately made Himself a symbol of the God-Son in man, showing how God-consciousness operates in an unknown psychological realm within each person. This realm He called the "Kingdom of God, or Heaven." He said, it is "within you." Today, psychologists call this realm the* unconscious *and acknowledge the reality of its existence.*

Jesus understood that truth flows with equal force in the *unconscious* of every person and is accessible when one seeks it in his inner kingdom. He knew how to reach this psychological realm and let its truth express through his voice and guide his drama. He realized that *truth alone reigns and governs,* freeing the individual from error.

But, more important, he understood that as truth comes into conscious expression among mankind, *Messiah comes into human expression,* bringing ever closer the golden age destined to manifest itself as truth takes over from error.

Jesus showed that neither the Jewish people nor their spiritual leaders will accept the fulfillment of *an externalized Messianic concept.* Consciously or unconsciously they know that all that Messiah represents cannot be vested in the frailty of Homo sapiens.[30] But *mankind* bears this seed, this promise, within him. Homo sapiens must, like Israel, bear this promise until the end of his days. It cannot be realized until a more mature expression of mankind comes into being through the evolution of consciousness, which must extend to include all of humanity. Man is still a childlike expression of what he is destined to be.

Jesus knew that many men before him had tried, but failed, to reverse Messianic expectation and turn mankind to look to itself, each seeking within himself for truth and working to establish an ethical society. Jesus turned the spotlight of history on the problem and its answer by dramatizing and symbolizing the Messianic complex and its psychological implications within the most intense expression of the complex in the world —in the midst of the Jewish people in Palestine. He knew what he was doing and was solely responsible for his death. *The Stranger* is saying that:

(1) The historical stand of the Jewish people has been correct. But he is also saying that Judaism must transcend its traditional Messianic expectation and *internalize* the concept. Only the concept of the coming of truth, full consciousness, and complete empathy to every individual—

which will in time insure the coming of the golden age—can contain the fullness of the promise that man has borne since the dawn of consciousness, symbolized in Adam-Eve. In accepting the concept of the *Inner* Messiah, Israel does not repudiate its historical role. Instead, it repudiates once and for all the political threat that realization of its externalized Messianic ideal inevitably and tacitly poses.

(2) St. Paul's concept of *saving grace coming to man* as the spirit of Jesus, *the Christ spirit*, entering into his consciousness is correct. Correct, because this spirit embodies full consciousness of oneself as Son of God, child of Cosmic mind and energy; this spirit expresses complete empathy with and love for all living things, seeing itself as brother to each human being; it is dedicated to seeking truth, acting honestly, accepting in "blind" faith if need be that man cannot be separated from the love of God or the life of the Cosmos, and this is "saving grace." But *The Stranger* is also saying that Christianity must accept Jesus' own evaluation of himself: a brother-being to the least person ever born, the same as he, without reservation, so that Jesus cannot be the "only Son of God," the only means of mankind's redemption. Christianity does not repudiate its historical role in *recognizing the whole story of the Son of man to be a symbolic representation of psychological factors and processes.* Instead, it repudiates once and for all the psychological threat that Jesus is when he is held to be purchaser, ransomer, judge, master over life and death, heaven or hell, for every person born on earth.

The meeting ground for Judaism and Christianity is: Judeo-Christian Depth Psychology. The Inner Messiah is ever coming to consciousness, but truth is also ever present in the "midst" of the individual, in his unknown psychological realm, the *unconscious*. The Messiah (Christ) symbolizes the inner psychic Authority which governs the life of the individual. This is the Authority-Ego which Jesus symbolized and spoke of in the name of *Son of man*.

In Jesus' dramatic revelation of the psyche, Israel represents the world of consciousness made up of a multitude of selves, past and present, so that in the realm of consciousness man has no "one ego" as such. He has an "ego-group."

From this ego-group are drawn the "elect of consciousness"—symbolized by the disciples—who respond to the invitation to do truth's work in consciousness. These are the "superego-group" and they act as liaison between consciousness and the *unconscious*, between Authority-Ego and its ego-group. This superego-group is not censuring and ascetic, harsh. It expresses in every degree love of life and man. Nor is it perfect. It demonstrates every *human* trait.

42

Conscience is symbolized by John the Baptist.

St. Paul and the figures that enter the drama in the New Testament symbolize the change that occurs in the world of consciousness after it has an encounter with its Authority-Ego, the Inner Messiah, Christ consciousness.

The dynamic processes of the psyche are revealed in the Bible when it is seen to be a symbolic revelation of the development of consciousness in man. The role of the Authority-Ego, Son of man, is detailed in the Gospels.

It is appropriate here to let another voice, from *Equals One*, the journal of Auroville, speak, because his words describe so well the "secret programming" in the psyche of each person that leads to fulfillment of the Messianic dream in the whole body of Mankind:

> Everything which has been promised in the old religions about the "second coming," about the "last avatar," the "twilight of the Gods," the "New Jerusalem"—this society would be able to manifest beyond our wildest dreams, because behind these dreams is a hidden truth, a secret programming in the human being which guides him through his evolution—the shadow of the light which the society of the future projected into our past. It was these dreams which slowly constituted the soul of mankind even before mankind had a bodily form. All our past has been only the foetal life of the society of the future, and each human being carries in himself this child of light, this secret programming, this dream. . . . We learn it gradually, and we have all eternity in which to prepare ourselves for those vast and intimate meetings of the future where we can exchange our whole fullness of being, of being human, with the whole fullness of being of everyone else.[31]

We will bring this scene to a close by giving you the A B C D of Jesus' message. It is:

TREMENDUM

History had arrived at the dividing point in calendar time, but only one person was aware of this. Standing at the crossroads of earth, he heard the converging tongues of humankind beseeching High Heaven as with one voice to fulfill man's ancient dream:

> "Oh, Holy One, come! Bring on the reign of God! Establish God's kingdom in this sorry world and right its wrongs! Save us!"

Then he spoke words that divided the calendar into before (B.C.) and after (A.D.) they were said. Here, in substance, is his message:

43

The reign of God is not coming as you expect it to come. No one will be able to say, "Here it is," or, "There it is." Behold, I say unto you, the reign of God is now in your midst. The kingdom of God is *within you.*

The Holy One is not coming as you expect him to come. In the kingdom within yourself you will find the Anointed One, God-Son, who speaks only in the name of God. And the name of God is *"One, I."* You see, "I" is God's *name* by which you call yourself. "I" is God's *name* by which I call myself. Although each of us is unique as an "only one," the name of God which we all bear, "I," binds us in the sameness of brotherhood.

Each of us has this One same measure of God's Parent Being within us, the same measure as I profess for myself. Even the lowliest or most despicable person, man or woman, has *it.* This One-God-measure is leader, teacher, Lord of each one's being, the Self of selves within him, upon whom the government of his life rests.

I will speak of this *One Self* of selves in each of us as *Son of man.* Listen well. When I speak of Son of man I speak of that of God which is within you and *is you*—of that of God which is within me and *is me*—of that within humankind which is divine, divinely guided, divinely human, divinely certain of everlasting life and love, purpose and satisfaction in being—of that which is full of power, glory, grace, and reality.

Son of man is that which is *tremendum* in each of us who was, or is ever to be, born: B.C. or A.D.

This is the A B C D of Jesus' message.

*   *   *   *   *

One moment, please! There's a question from the audience. The young lady in the first row—your name?

> "My name is Eve. Why *Son* of man, if
> woman, too, has *it?* Why not *Child* of man?"

This question is answered in Section XIII of Book II of *The Single Reality,* the Book titled, *If Thine Eye Be Single.* But we may deal with it briefly here.

In life's beginning, only femaleness was present. This is to say, the first

44

living cells that divided to become two must be seen as "daughter cells." In time, these cells began to reproduce through means of a process that is today called parthenogenesis, which typically involves the development of eggs from virgin females without fertilization by spermatozoa. When parthenogenesis is accomplished in laboratory experiments, only female offspring are produced.

We do not know how long in life's history femaleness reproduced only itself. Or what happened in the cross-action of the nuclei of female cells that produced the first male. We do know today that *all* mammalian embryos are anatomically female during the early stages of fetal life. Therefore, each of us *begins in femaleness*—just as life began.

A new generation entered into life with the advent of maleness. Each of us, regardless of our gender, is a part of maleness because our bodies are sexually conceived by means of spermatozoa fertilizing ova.

In order to correspond to biological fact, the creation story would have to tell of femaleness preceding maleness, of Adam's being drawn from Eve, if Adam is seen simply as a male. But the story says: "In the day that God created man, in the likeness of God made he him; Male and female created he them; and blessed them, and called their name Adam, in the day when they were created." (Gen. 5:1-2).

From the beginning, mankind was Adam-Eve, a correspondence to the hydrogen molecule in which two whole ones share a field. What the creation story tells us is that *Eve is of the new generation drawn from maleness*—Woman is as Adam, constituted as is Man.

Adam, in the beginning, must be seen as representation of a "body of consciousness" that expresses its own physical body to which it is mated until death. Inherent in both the consciousness and the physical body is maleness and femaleness, regardless of sex—as was the case with Adam. Mankind, maleness, able to produce male or female offspring, is life's triumphant generation. Since all of us are of that generation, we are "brother-beings."

And Son energy, the Son-Self of God within us, is the Authority we possess which is *tremendum*—is that of which Jesus spoke when he spoke of Son of man.

The razor's edge, which each of us must walk, begins as the power and glory of this Authority, the Inner Messiah, stirs in our depths and, to greater or lesser degree, enters into our conscious expression. Let us turn attention now to this aspect of mankind.

The Threat and the Blessing of
Messianic Pretension and Messianic Delusion

As we return to *The Shining Stranger*, we find that the theme of the Messianic dream, the "secret programming" of the Inner Messiah which each person carries within himself, threads its course throughout the book.

The Messianic complex has been the "secret programmer" of history, individual and social. Its effect can be devastating, leading to insane and criminal expression which can be as far-reaching as Hitler's. But the effect of the Messianic compulsion that arises in the individual can also lead him to be society's great benefactor. Dr. Abraham Maslow says that all really serious men are Messianic, having no interest in anything but their mission.[32] Such men are the "growing tip" of the human species and are responsible for the evolution of its consciousness as well as its social systems.

Jesus saw that because each person carries the Messianic promise within himself, each is subject to Messianic pretension and delusion. He realized that only when the Messianic complex is understood is its social and psychological threat mitigated; and through such understanding, the constructive potential inherent in the ideal is released.

The Messianic complex expresses itself in two ways:

(1) As the will to power, exerted to deliver the world from what the self-styled Messiah sees to be evil, or to save man from himself, in one way or another reserving power to the few, the sufferer himself becoming master. Such will to power leads to Messianic pretension and the delusion that the pretender has been strangely and uniquely selected by Providence to fill the role.

(2) As the need to express the truth one has grasped, in the firm conviction that he alone possesses it and can save the world through somehow forcing attention upon it, even if this requires his own martyrdom.

46

This leads to Messianic delusion, and the sufferer's self-sought persecution. In one way or another, he demands his own crucifixion and gives his life for the message he would convey.

As a rule, both aspects of the Messianic complex are expressed simultaneously, one or the other predominating to greater or lesser degree. Each aspect is a perversion of truth. Each person is uniquely endowed to exert his power to deliver the world from evil; but this power does not extend beyond the Lilliputian ability to secure one cord upon the Gulliver of society; and that one cord binds the person's own measure of evil. Each person must also express the truth as he sees it; but the only thing unique about the truth he possesses is his mode of expressing it; and no one person can express the whole of truth; insanity overtakes him to the degree that he attempts to do this.

Jesus understood and revealed in his drama every facet of the Messianic complex. *The Stranger* says that Jesus could not have done so unless he had suffered it himself, because from birth the belief that he was Messiah had been implanted in his mind by his parents and the small group who shared their conviction.[33]

But Jesus' failure to respond to Satan's "tempting," and Jesus' consistent repudiation of the prevailing concepts of what Messiah was to be, what he was to do, indicate that as the forces of the Messianic complex culminated in him, he recognized its insanity and recovered from it before he began his ministry. In this ministry, he "ransomed the righteous"—because *expression of the Messianic complex always begins in righteousness.*

History is full of noble reformers, truth bearers, world savers, whose righteousness and search for truth leads them to their own destruction or the destruction of their sanity and then to devastating acts upon themselves or in society. Jesus relieved the righteous of the necessity to play the Messianic role because it was finished in his person—its self-sought martyrdom revealed. He broke the mold in which the ancient Messianic expression, as the will to power in this world, could be cast. And he fashioned the "mold of righteousness" to take the shape of: servant to one's fellowman and truth, commitment to the ethic of love, empathy (compassion), and honesty. He emphasized that the Messianic man must see himself to be no more, no less, endowed with truth and power than the lowliest of his fellowmen.

Jesus saw that sooner or later each person must struggle with the Messianic complex because sooner or later each person becomes aware of and must struggle with the promptings of the power vested in him. Until mankind realizes that the God-Son is born in every babe, that each is endowed with one full, equal measure of truth and power—and that each is governed and guided by his own Inner Messiah who "programs" his life through time, so that his evolution into wholeness and glory is assured—man and society will suffer the ravages of the Messianic complex.

When the realization comes that each is One, Son, equally endowed, a person is reborn in consciousness. The need to "save the world" has left him and he "labors humbly in Truth's vineyard, awaiting the grace of nature, knowing that life has given itself, its voice, to man and for man."[34] Love of life, joy in living in ways both great and small, becomes *pure* worship, unsullied by false piety and the vicariousness that an externalized Messianic concept demands. The wisdom of Zen is expressed here. And a person needs a teacher because, as *The Stranger* says, "a man must grasp the Christ (truth) in another, and realize the Christ to be in all men, before he can realize the truth of its being in himself and sustain this realization in sanity."[35] Each must choose his own teacher, who expresses truth in his person and leads his pupil into its paths. Teacher, servant of truth, is what Jesus stated himself to be. This is what he saw every person to be who worships in spirit and in truth.

Every great religious figure in history is such a teacher. The day of the fulfillment of the prophecy of Micah draws nearer. The world begins to recognize the *underlying psychological truth* that gives rise to religious expression in every tongue, however the *name* of God or teacher be called. Hear the words of Micah:

> For all people will walk every one in the name of his God, and we will walk in the name of the Lord our God for ever and ever.[36]

This, our generation, needs a new name for God, a new name for Teacher. We understand better the magnificence of the Cosmos and of universal energy in its least and most far-flung expression. Should our new name for God be: Cosmos? And we understand better that the great Teacher must be above all a very *human* being, artist of life in his love for its every expression. Should our new name for Teacher be: Humanism? *Cosmic Humanism*, the name, the new name, for emergent Religion?

The Stranger does not offer this name for the unifying concept of God and man that Harold's book invites. Preston Harold had left the play before Oliver Reiser's book came upon the scene. Reiser's work is not mentioned by him, but the attitude and approach of the two authors is compatible. *The Stranger* speaks of *Christian Realism*,[37] and we must hear his answer to other facets of the Palestinian mystery play in order to understand what he meant by this term.

The Sacred Books of Each Religion
Are the True Historical Messiahs

The Stranger says that "although Jesus, Himself, was not historical Messiah, through His work the Bible, itself historical Judaic Messiah, came into the world, its content delivered by the pen of the Jewish race. . . . The Bible is not the unquestionable word of God; it is the now unshakable work of men giving expression to consciousness of God in their being. . . . It is the Bible of human consciousness. . . ."[38]

The Stranger is saying that the Bible fulfills the Judaic promise to bring the truth of man into expression in this world—and this truth itself is the governing factor. Through the Bible, Judaic Messianic expectation has been fulfilled. In it, Christian Messianic expectation vested in the second coming of Jesus has been fulfilled; because through the Gospels Jesus returned to the domain of men, speaking with the same authority that marked his ministry, and this happened during the lifetime of the "beloved" disciple.

But what of the Messianic expectations of the rest of the world? *The Stranger* says that truth speaks the same words in every tongue. Therefore, each great religion must rightfully treasure its own Objectified Messiah, its Sacred Book, through which truth is brought to man's consciousness in every generation. Jesus recognized this, and in the formulating of his doctrine drew upon the treasured writings of all mankind. But he could not mention them by name. Why?

Jesus realized that each religious figure who preceded him and each that followed must himself become the being-symbol of the individual's psyche in order to convey psychological truth. The being-symbol must represent the Authority-Ego in the individual's *own world of consciousness*. Therefore, such a symbol could speak only *of himself* and *to his own people*. In order to be a true symbol of the Authority-Ego in each person, Jesus could address himself only to Israel, his own "ego-group."

Each such symbol must speak in the name of "I" if he would speak in the name of *One*, God, Cosmos.

Therefore, in *The Stranger*'s view, as each person takes a new view of his own faith, he will find the symbols that match the structure of personality which are found in the Judeo-Christian tradition; and he will find the revelation of essentially the same dynamic psychic processes that Harold describes, following the course of *Son of man* in the Gospels.

Christian Realism will lead Christianity to realize that it cannot explain away the Gospels. If they were written in the way that scholars now propose—many years after Jesus' death, dependent upon the failing memories of old men, the accounts changed or slanted, so that the real message of Jesus breaks through only here and there almost in spite of, rather than because of, the men who recorded his story—then Christianity is founded upon a mythical character.

The Stranger says that the Gospels were not tampered with. But how accurate can the Gospels be? In ordinary course, much of what Jesus said could not have been remembered, even as it was spoken. Harold could not accept the view that God pushed the pen of the authors any more surely than God pushes the pen of every person who writes a word on any subject. *The Stranger* deals only with that which is natural, not supranatural. Every interpretation is based upon, measured against, evidence within the realm of demonstrable phenomena.

Harold saw that the only known way in which the Gospels could convey the very words of Jesus, giving real substance to the record upon which Christianity rests, is by Jesus' use of hypnotism, through which he could be assured that his disciples would *remember* what he told them to record and would follow his instructions regarding the bringing forth of the Gospels.

Jesus using hypnotism? Hypnotism!

Withhold judgment, please. Do not turn away from the word *hypnosis*. Read Harold's handling of the subject in *The Shining Stranger*. More will be said about it later in our Play.

The important point we would make here—the point we hope you will remember—is: Harold believed that Jesus understood psychic power and its use to as great a degree as Homo sapiens can, although Jesus himself said that others would perform greater works than he did. At the level of Jesus' understanding, and the consequent way he exercised psychic power, his use of the hypnotic means cannot be thought of in the way we, with our limited understanding, usually think of the practice. Jesus' practice, his understanding, so far transcends this that Harold used the word *hypnotism* only because there is no other word that provides as good a frame of reference within which to explore and examine the many mysterious workings of man's mental, psychic, and physical energy.

As for these strange workings, here we will say only that it is a well-known fact that a person in trance can remember what he is told to remember; and he will follow the suggestions or commands given, long after he has wakened. He may not know why he feels compelled to act as he has been instructed to act—regardless of how irrational his behavior seems to himself or others—but he will perform as told to perform unless the instructions are contrary to his very basic commitments.

The disciples themselves may not have understood their own behavior in the "birthing" of Jesus' record. The veil that was drawn to shroud this nativity—the disappearance of the original "Q" source and the "M" and "L" elaborations, the tolerance, each for the other's version of what happened—was a part of the plan Jesus made to insure his return through the advent of these documents, and, at the same time, *to lay down the pattern of how the words of truth that issue from a person's Authority-Ego are conveyed into his conscious domain.* Here is the pattern:

Jesus, symbol of Authority-Ego, wrote nothing. The disciples, symbol of the superego that bridges the conscious and *unconscious* domains, conveyed Jesus' words and drama to the world. We see that the Authority-Ego does not communicate directly. Because the message must be conveyed through the superego, which is involved with conscious knowledge and fantasy to some degree, at best there will be a modicum of interpolation, distortion, and adulteration of the message that is conveyed. Remember this as you ponder the messages of prophets and oracles, modern or ancient, wondering how accurate they may be. Through Jesus' use of posthypnotic recall, this threat to his message was reduced to an absolute minimum—another reason for utilizing this means—and the psychic pattern of how the words of the God-Son in man come into expression was laid down.

The amount of information that can be apprehended by Homo sapiens' consciousness is limited. When man questions beyond his ability to understand the answer, or when he questions in terms too broad, or when the question itself is composed of error, the answer must be given in parable, allegory, metaphor, or symbolic form. And the answer must be given in the terms in which the question was posed, just as an algebraic problem must be worked utilizing the given set of symbols.

The Stranger says that Jesus chose for disciples men who were neither intellectuals nor mystics. He committed them to the one task of conveying his message as the "spirit" (psychic power) brought remembrance. Harold points out that Jesus, too, must speak through his own superego as he went into trance and let "I" reveal itself through his voice. The message he gave the world is eternally fresh in meaning because Jesus was committed in consciousness to the natural in life and to the discipline of mathematics. His parables follow nature's path and the channels of everyday living, or they are given in the language of arithmetic, which everyone can understand.

The most important thing Jesus had to do was to insure that in the Gospels he would be presented as a true symbol of the Authority-Ego in man, with its Christ-consciousness. Here, we must face the question of why the Gospels are so contradictory. They differ even in the matter of the length of Jesus' ministry.

In Harold's view, *Jesus saw to it that the Gospels would contradict each other in many ways, on many levels, in order to symbolize the psychic truth that the coming of Son-consciousness into a person's conscious mind cannot be forced into a chronological pattern applicable to everyone. Nor can the operation of Son-consciousness be formalized into a given pattern. It comes and goes in different ways, at different times, and stays for different durations in those who express it. But, sooner or later, it comes to everyone.*

Jesus did not attempt to convey the whole of truth. He called upon the Scriptures, and he called upon the psychic power of other men to help him. He told his disciples that the *holy spirit would bring remembrance* of all he had said to them.[39] Here, he clearly indicated his use of the means of posthypnotic recall.

In Jesus' day, psychic power was called "spirit." Hypnotism is exertion of psychic power. Harold believed that Jesus understood this power as few have before or since and that he demonstrated and revealed its every aspect. An enlightened world must examine this extraordinary power that, when understood, could be the greatest of blessings. Coming onto the scene is a generation that is not afraid of the idea of psychic power and demands to know more about it. But even to them hypnotism is apt to be a distasteful subject—we need a new name for it.

Whatever we may think of hypnosis, *the idea that Jesus employed the natural power of posthypnotic response to suggestion to insure that his message be given as he wished to give it is a completely new answer to the mystery of the Gospels.*

It is also an answer that undoes a century of "Form Criticism" and

"Jesus Research." This ragged rug is pulled out from under a Christianity that is largely an apology for Jesus, because Christians can no longer really believe the Pauline interpretation of him. Young and old are understandably disenchanted with traditional theology, Judaic and Christian. Western religion literally finds itself between the devil and the deep blue sea.

On the one hand, there are the fundamentalists, who cling to the image of God and the Bible that is dead or dying in our time—wrathful Jehovah, heaven and hell, the devil tempting humankind, angels dictating every word of the Holy Writ.

On the other hand, there are the sophisticated scholars, who have researched the Bible to death, pronouncing the Gospels to be an unreliable record of Jesus. They seem to forget that there is *no other record*. If the Gospels are not a valid account of Jesus, there is no *reason* for Christianity to continue to exist; it must follow that Christianity is founded upon no more than a literary character drawn from conglomerate and contradictory views. Theologians, take note: Christianity is drowning in the morass that "Form Criticism" and "Jesus Research" has made of the Gospels.

We have said this before. But it is worth repeating. Jesus and the Gospels are indivisible—the one as valid as the other, the one as easily explained away as the other.

There is an answer that transcends the dilemma, an answer that confounds the "devil" and escapes the "deeps." Harold gave it.

The Gospels truly bring Jesus to life when we view them as the product of man's ability to remember correctly what he is told to remember in trance. The integrity of the disciples in relating Jesus' drama as they participated in it and as each was told to convey it is established. It also becomes clear that any valid interpretation of Jesus must be based upon his *own words* as given in the Gospels—not upon St. Paul's interpretation of him. *The Stranger* takes its stand upon Jesus' words.

Jesus spoke strange words, which did not appear to be fulfilled. He said to his questioners that they would *all* see the Son of man descending upon the clouds of heaven.[40] To the early Christians, this event would herald the end of the world.

How does *The Stranger* handle this predicament that beset Christianity from its beginning? We shall deal with this in Scene IV.

Return of the Son of Man
Is a Subjective Reality Fulfilled at Death—
A Part of Jesus' Doctrine of Reincarnation

Son of man means simply *man*. It is the name Jesus used to identify himself as *symbol* of the psychic factor that Harold calls the Authority-Ego, God-Son in the unconscious psychic realm, whose return heralds the end of the world. When will this happen?

The end of this world comes for each individual at death.

Jesus' words say that this psychic factor, Son of man, Self-of-selves, full of glory, grace, and reality—this Self-knowing—descends upon the "clouds of heaven," *which means the clouds of inner space*, reuniting with its ego-group or world of consciousness at death. Then, on another plane of being, and in the womb, the "secret programming" of one's life that will bring him to fruition in evolution's process, whatever the hue that lifetime takes, continues.

The term *unconscious* is an unfortunate choice for the innermost depths and outermost reaches of the human psyche. This realm is unknown, but it is not unknowing. Because Jesus knew how to set his consciousness aside and let universal truth speak from the depths of his psyche, he could reveal man's nature and the psychic operations that take place in the inner kingdom. The "clouds of heaven" indicate the subjective nature of Jesus' words. *By pointing out the subjective nature of the end of the world, Harold resolves the apparent contradiction between what Jesus said and his failure to return as expected. The psychic factor, Son of man, returns at death.*

Only a few face death with open eyes or are able to indicate what happens. When Stephen, the first Christian martyr, was dying, he opened his eyes and cried out, "Look, I see the heavens opened, and the Son of man standing on the right hand of God." In April, 1967, when Aaron

54

Mitchell was executed in San Quentin Prison, as he was dying he screamed, "I'm Jesus Christ." Jesus said that the least person on earth must be seen to be the *same as himself.* Harold believed that this realization comes at death, although few are able to communicate it.

In *The Stranger's* view, Jesus deliberately prohibited any description of his physical appearance being recorded in the Gospels. He did this in order that he might become a symbol of the Self of any person, and his entire drama might become a pattern of the psychological operation within the unknown inner kingdom.

If Son of man comes at death to gather his world of consciousness into the inner fold, what then? What of heaven and hell?

Jesus promised neither. Indeed, he said that *heaven* and earth would pass away.[41] Jesus promised eternal *life* and said that God *had* committed mankind to this: ". . . the Father raises the dead and makes them live. . . ." —"Ye must be born again."[42] This, clearly, simply, is the doctrine of reincarnation.

Centuries ago the doctrine of reincarnation was edited out of Christian theology. But the Gospels permit no editing. Throughout, they proclaim everlasting life—to be realized step by step as the childlike expression of man, that Homo sapiens is, matures in consciousness. Life cannot become eternal until mankind through learning develops incorruptible consciousness that will lead to his generating incorruptible flesh. Then the pendulum between life and death will move evenly with no loss of consciousness —death will be in life as sleeping and waking are in life. Heaven, the *unconscious,* will have passed away, because its truth will have come into conscious expression. Earth, the body, *passes away while it is in its living state,* as its cells divide, replenish, and renew it.

Homo sapiens' limited consciousness cannot envision a future state of being that will correspond altogether with the reality of it. Even the "earth" of this generation of man, his flesh, will have passed away as his ever-enlarging consciousness constructs a new temple of being to house itself in a body that will constantly be made anew.

We are just beginning to learn how completely consciousness controls the flesh. It was Jesus' understanding of this and his understanding of the involvement of psychic energy in normal perception, that led to his demonstrations which seem miraculous. These will be discussed later. It is enough to say here that man cannot answer the being-question until he comprehends the limits of his natural powers and understands death as a part of the process of his ongoing life until evolution reaches its goal: life everlasting.

Jesus said that each person "hath one" that judges him—God does not judge man.[43] The Son-Self in man judges his own world of selves, carrying on in the inner kingdom all he has known of love, truth, joy—returning to life that part of himself which he has found wanting, to experience good and evil in order that he may become conscious of life as it operates in truth and reality. And with each rebirth, a person brings into life a measure of himself that has yet to experience life. In his inner kingdom, the living images of all he has loved continue as a part of his very own being and eternal life. The understanding he has gained can never be lost. As he moves through his many lives, his evil attenuates and is recast, turning in the end to laughter or humor (ask a psychologist what laughter is "made of").

The Stranger says:

> Just as the child cannot love beyond the limitations imposed by his immaturity, so Homo sapiens cannot love beyond loving another *as himself*. As the beloved's image becomes a part of himself in being, the beloved's essence is experienced, but not possessed. Like a child, Homo sapiens enfolds the promise of knowing a different kind of love as he reaches maturity. With whom will he know it, share it? With the incomparable of himself made of *all* he has known of love. Nothing other can satisfy him eternally and be perfectly at home in his own world and being. This is not to suggest that the hope of reunion with others is false. It is to suggest that each becomes an eternal and essential part of another who has loved him, and he will recognize himself in that person; just as another he has loved becomes an eternal part of himself, and will recognize himself as an essential part of one's own love. One *keeps* one's loves. As to that which he loses, in Shakespeare's words, "Nothing of him that doth fade, but doth suffer a sea-change into something rich and strange." Beyond this, the "dimensions of heaven" cannot be mapped. . . . Man's first creative act is to fashion from his life experience a complementary-being: a personality he truly loves, born of and incorporating all he has loved. . . . Man is to possess a new *sense* of being: a companion-sense in life born of love itself. . . . Today, man senses his "I-being"—in some tomorrow he will sense "us-being" when the love he has known in life twice glorifies him.[44]

Son of man is "I-being" which *perfectly understands the frailty of its conscious soul*, and comes at death *to gather its ego-group in loving embrace, as a "bridegroom" comes to his bride.*

Jesus does not qualify the nature of this coming—whatever the hue of one's life, Son of man gathers the soul in loving compassion. There need be no fear of death itself. (And when man understands that nature has provided him the means of perfect anesthesia through exercise of auto-hypnosis—about which more will be said later—there need be no fear of the pain that may be attendant upon dying.) Death brings one's very own beloved Self of selves.

The uncertainty of the hour of one's death matches the uncertainty of the hour of the returning Son of man, as Jesus described it.[45] He said that the many who would come in his name were not to be believed, and left no indication that he as person would ever return in recognizable form.[46] But he had to describe the psychic dynamic of death: self-union with one's own Divine Absence, which is ever present on the other side of the mask he wears as he plays his role.

The Western world seems ready to accept the principle of rebirth, reincarnation. It corresponds with man's sense of justice and fits into the pattern of the evolution of consciousness. Much fantasy attaches to the idea, and this will continue until the study of man's consciousness throws more light upon the subject. Mankind may have *fetal knowledge* of reincarnation, which gives rise to his feeling of the certainty of life. This knowledge may be accessible—the facts of life might be gleaned—if man will seek first the kingdom within as he seeks the truth of his being. Hypnosis presents itself. In trance, a person can be regressed in time, perhaps into the womb. But, in Harold's view, not beyond. He believed that we should explore only within the discernible limits, from conception to death; and not for the purpose of seeking knowledge of our pasts, but for the purpose of understanding, and gaining guidance for the future.

Reincarnation confronts man with the necessity to make *this world* a better place to live in if he hopes to come into a "better hereafter." Jesus' concern was with this world, and his teaching leads men toward establishing an ethical society in which mankind may have life and have it abundantly. This is his own statement as to why he was doing what he did.

The Miracles Are Demonstrations of Psychic Power

The play of energy in man's inner space accounts for the miracles, and Harold relates that play to hypnosis. That stumbling block of a word again!

Harold chose to use the word *hypnotism* because all too many scientists refuse to admit that any form of ESP or psi-power exists. What else but the exercise of psychic power accounts for hypnotic phenomena? The most skeptical scientist cannot deny that an unknown range of hypnotic states can be produced, and the phenomena occurring in such states can be repeated. In discussing the data of hypnosis, Willis W. Harman says:[47]

Of all those phenomena whose existence is widely recognized by scientists (whether or not they are felt to be understood), among the most fraught with significance and implication are those associated with hypnosis. The basic facts are generally known, but we have hesitated to draw the conclusions to which they point. A recent inventory of scientific findings about human behavior (Berelson & Steiner, 1964, pp. 121–123) lists a number of established findings regarding hypnosis, including the following:

Hypnotism works: that is, there is no question today that hypnotism can induce all of the following "unnatural" states:

1. anesthesia and analgesia, local or general
2. positive and negative hallucinations
3. regression to an earlier age
4. unusual muscular strength, rigidity, resistance to fatigue
5. organic effects, normally outside voluntary control. . . .

For example, a hypnotized subject may be induced to perceive an imaginary kitten placed in her lap. She experiences stroking the kitten and hearing it purr; the senses of sight, touch, and hearing seem to corroborate the hypnotist's suggestion. Yet this is a "positive hallucination." There is no kitty there.

Other examples are familiar. A subject accepts the suggestion that a person sitting in a particular chair really is not there; he perceives an empty chair. . . . Blisters and burned spots can be produced by hypnotic suggestion. . . . By changing the way in which [an] individual perceived the world his depth perception, time perception, movement perception, color perception, and so on, major behavior changes, as well as mental states ranging from psychoticlike to euphoric and mystical, were produced.

In combining the study of all paranormal phenomena into the study of the hypnotic state, Harold brings his reader into immediate contact with undeniable reality and provides a framework within which the miracles can be studied.

In the hypnotic state, the effects that Harman lists as well as many others—some strange indeed—can be produced, so that the range of possibilities is extremely wide. In Harold's view, the range of the hypnotic state is also wider than it is usually considered to be. The hypnotic state is simply a state of trance, which can be anything from a momentary lapse of awareness, or "shift" of consciousness, to deathlike coma. The dynamics of inducing trance or the hypnotic state are outlined as Harold begins his discussion of the miracles. Although he does not necessarily rule out all other explanations, he shows that *all the miracles can be seen to be demonstrations within the known limits of hypnotic phenomena,* so that all of them fall within the realm of natural happenings.

The Stranger urges that research by medical men and psychologists be broadened, and that everything that is known about hypnosis be made common knowledge. Throughout history the power to employ hypnosis has been used—and often abused by design or through ignorance of its effects. It is a natural power which mankind must understand because man is subject to its use and misuse from birth to death. Harman puts it well:

> Now what are the conditions essential to the production of hypnotic phenomena? In their barest simplicity, they are (1) a source of suggestion and (2) the willingness, at a deep level in the personality, to accept suggestion from that source. But surely these conditions are met in our infancy and early childhood. . . . The inference is as obvious as it is startling: *We are all hypnotized from infancy.*

Today, it is thought that a person under the hypnotic control of another cannot be made to do anything that is actually against his will or contrary to his desires. But we do not know for sure. We do know that when a person does respond by accepting suggestion, he is expressing *his own will* and willingness to cooperate at the deep levels of his being.

It is difficult, if not impossible, to hypnotize an *unwilling* subject—although not necessarily an unaware subject.

Scientists must determine whether a person can be made to act against his own will in the hypnotic state. If so, young people must be taught the dynamics of hypnosis—how to recognize hypnotic tactics and defend against them. Power of any sort may be constructively used, or it may be misused. The more subtle the power, the more susceptible it is to misuse and also *the greater is its potential to produce beneficial effects.*

Because we know that the person who responds to suggestion is expressing his own will and willingness to cooperate, it must follow that Jesus' disciples were not "used" or "misused" or "controlled" by him. They were his willing co-workers in his mission to reveal the nature of man and the power with which he is endowed.

Harold says that Jesus showed the effects that can be produced through exercise of psychic power in man—*its ability to delude as well as to illuminate*—and he demonstrated the release of the body's own healing power in hypnotic trance.[48]

Harold designated the hypnotic state as any state in which the person is not normally alert and concentrating *intellectually* upon whatever he is doing. Trance may be self-induced, induced by another, or it may come spontaneously. In certain trance states, if not in all such states, something other than normal consciousness takes over—and miraculous feats, physical and otherwise, may be accomplished without apparent effort.

The whole story of hypnosis is a story of miracles and failure to perform miracles—of use and misuse, of possibilities so wide that *all* mysterious phenomena can be related to it or produced through use of it. It is necessary that man understand the power of hypnosis because it is *a part of his natural endowment.* He may use this power beneficially or to the detriment of himself and others. This is why, according to *The Stranger,* Jesus showed in his works and described as best he could in the language of his day the dynamics of this power. Man cannot understand himself until he understands it; he cannot reach his full potential and a new plateau of freedom until he knows how to defend against its misuse and use it himself to meet countless needs. For example, he could use it to produce anesthesia, without use of drugs, which in cases of long illness often lead to traumatic side effects; he could use it to easily "program" his mind with data he needs to remember.

But again and again, Harold stresses the point that Jesus made in his every demonstration of psychic power: it is not itself a "cure" for anything, not a panacea on which man may depend for the working of "miracles" to meet his needs. With every use of this power, there is that within man (his own Authority-Ego) which demands that *he take a corresponding step in exhibiting conscious control of himself*. He can accomplish this only as his consciousness of truth and reality also widens. He must understand that something he is expressing in his conscious or subconscious mind, in his behavior or emotional responses, has led him into his predicament or created his need in the first instance.

It is appropriate to say here that Harold believed the necessity for further research in hypnosis and psychic phenomena should in no way lessen or diminish further research in regular medical practice such as surgery and the development of beneficial drugs. Mankind should utilize all the blessings and knowledge that medicine has put within reach.

It remains true, however, that the advances medicine has made have served inevitably to deepen man's understanding that mind and body are inseparable. To an ever-enlarging degree it is apparent that the mind and emotions control the flesh and the health of the human being. *The Stranger* says that medical men are becoming ever more aware that restoring health and prolonging life is not in itself enough. The physician must restore meaning to the life of the patient:

> The sickness besetting man's soul cannot be healed by medical science or by hypnotherapy—this illness is caused by loss of religion, which gives rise to a decline in one's sense of purpose and meaning in life, and to unspoken despair. . . . To the twentieth century, Jesus' words still say: "If thou canst believe, all things are possible to him that believeth . . ." And like the father of the tormented child, this century cries out and says with tears: "Lord, I believe; help thou mine unbelief." Today, as always, "mine unbelief" is the sickness that must first be healed.

Harold said that as the biblical miracles are considered, a person should not dwell upon how much he knows that makes it impossible for them to be true. He should think about how little he knows to make it possible for him to understand them and *describe* them in the scientific terms he now demands. A miracle cannot be *willed*, and belief, doubting not, is the most difficult of all psychological states to induce when a person is in dire distress—it is doubtful if anyone could muster sufficient faith unless he could lose his conscious fear in a blessed state of trance.

To those who could receive it, Jesus imparted his own faith. But he pointed to an easier way than seeking a miracle for a person to meet his every need, saying that we must seek first the inner kingdom of God and his righteousness. Today, we seek this inner realm, but we call this the practice of depth psychology.

The Stranger says that in today's world it would be a miracle if anyone could fulfill the conditions Jesus outlined. Yet miraculous faith healings take place. Katherine Kuhlman, for example, somehow helps many in her audiences to release fear and accept the healing evoked by the "holy spirit of God"—the spiritual or psychic energy with which man is endowed—as she stands, a shining example of faith, before thousands of people to whom she imparts it in varying degree.

But for all too many, fear of derision, or knowledge of the "impossibility" of the situation, prevent expression of faith. The medical fraternity could create the climate in which it would not be so difficult to release fear and to put aside the intellectual knowledge that stifles hope. They could send teams to study the great faith healers living today to try to determine the psychic principle that is being employed, no doubt with many variations.

We, the audience, must insist that such a mysterious and uneducated "medic" as Arigo of Brazil be studied while he is living and practicing medicine so successfully—at the same time defying much that today is standard medical practice. He employs both surgery and drugs but ignores antiseptic measures. He uses no narcotic anesthesia, but his patients feel no pain. He "closes" incisions with his hands—not stitches —and they remain closed and heal. Some medical men are courageous enough to undertake serious study of such healers. Dr. Andrija Puharich is one who has made trips to Brazil to study Arigo and film his work.[49] Arigo must induce trance rapidly and unobtrusively to produce anesthesia in his patients as he operates so swiftly, using a small unsterile knife. No infection follows. Long ago in India, Dr. James Esdaile, learned surgeon, used hypnosis to induce anesthesia and performed hundreds of major operations with very little postoperative infection. Edgar Cayce went into deep trance before taking his journeys into the bodies of faraway patients to diagnose and prescribe treatment—these were psychic probes that caused no pain.

Well, let us look now at Jesus, the healer. He said that others would do greater deeds than he did—thereby ruling out the idea that God worked through him in a supranatural way.

Harold points out that the type of illnesses Jesus cured are limited and that he told people their own faith, belief, *expectation* had made them whole. He did not effect a healing every time he attempted to cure, or else he did not attempt all the cases he was expected to cure. In his home territory where he was known as the son of the carpenter and was without prestige, he could not perform many miracles of healing. The dynamics he used follow the well-established pattern of releasing the body's healing power in hypnotic trance, wherein the prestige of the operator plays an important role and the patient's own expectations and wishes (conscious or subconscious) determine his response to suggestion.

We must remember that the operator's beliefs, prejudices, expectations also play an important role and that the ability to induce trance or to go into trance state varies widely. But there is more than this involved. Some *principle* is being touched upon, and we must discover it. What was the secret of Jesus' success?

Harold saw that something must break the grip of fear before healing power can be released. Trance, however light and fleeting, provides a moment's mental or physical anesthesia, so that *anesthesia itself* might be the healing secret. He saw also that the patient must somehow be "shocked" into making his response, but the shock must not be too traumatic if it is to be fully effective. There are many kinds of anesthesia, beginning with words of reassurance. There are many kinds of shock, beginning with surprising words or unexpected authoritative commands. Harold believed the principle involved a play between anesthesia and shock which in itself can produce anesthesia.

Consider for a moment that spontaneous remission of the most hopeless cases of cancer is the great mystery researchers face. Might some type of shock be involved?

"Is there a doctor in the house? If so, will he come to the stage and tell us if research is being done in shock therapy for treatment of cancer? Has anyone tried electric anesthesia, which produces both unconsciousness and what might be called total physical shock? Might sleep treatment hold promise?"

"Will a psychologist step forward and tell us whether hypnotists are attempting to discover in Mesmer's records what *principle* he employed, although he may not have understood himself what he was doing?

63

Could he have been so successful because he reinforced verbal suggestion with physical touch, or motions that directed attention upon the ailing part of the body?"

"I'm wondering about some sort of shock therapy for mentally retarded children—to wake them up—somehow they seem to be in a sort of sleep. There are so many who have no discernible brain damage. Could a retarded child be hypnotized?"

Let us have order, please! The best we can do to answer your questions is to look again at Jesus' method of healing. *The Stranger* suggests that Jesus went quickly into trance himself, leading his patients into the hypnotic state so swiftly that the observers were unaware of what was actually happening. Inducing the desired state of trance is not easily done.

Harold says, "To go into trance, a person must have *faith in the operator.* Consciousness of man's fallibility and knowledge of the operator limit this faith. . . ." And insofar as expectation or faith that a healing will take place is concerned, reason and intellectual conditioning limit faith. "Thus, the limits of faith that it is possible to possess *in reality* limit the effectiveness of hypnotherapy, which may, *theoretically*, be without limit in its application, but in reality is limited because reason limits faith. As one reviews the healings of Jesus when the patient was there and conscious, one sees a pattern of:

Rapid induction into trance.
Authoritative command or surprising word to produce a degree of shock, coupled with a physical factor, such as touch or stretching forth the hand, *to reinforce and direct verbal suggestion.* Therapy is administered by an operator devoid of ego-group in play [the Authority-Ego, the Christ-factor, is the only psychic factor in Jesus that is active in the process]; the patient is given over to the forces within him; faith is the determining factor. . . .

. . . The image Jesus formed and projected was the Christ of God in man which makes him whole and perfect. . . . Through this symbol, Jesus

healed: . . . the symbol of Self as 'Divine Child'. . . . His secret appears
to rest in knowing that only the Christ which is in man can perform
the miracle of a true and lasting healing. . . . Jesus warned that the
approach is broad, but the way is narrow. Each may have a secret 'loop
hole' through which he enters the state of sleep or trance—both conditions could be differing degrees of anesthesia which permits the self-
healing power to operate. . . ."

Again and again, Harold stresses that the problem is to discover the
principle Jesus employed—*the call he made on a person's consciousness
and unconscious forces, because the process involves a change in both
these dimensions of one's being.* It is to be hoped that aversion to the
word *hypnotism* will not prevent a careful study of that principle as *The
Stranger* details it.

This is especially important in those cases when Jesus' patients did not
come into immediate contact with him. Three such healings are reported.
In these cases *The Stranger* says that Jesus demonstrated extrasensory
perception and showed that telepathic communication can be directed
through a medium to heal a patient who is not present.

As for raising the dead—raising the *dead*! Doctors do it today, sometimes using means that might well kill the living. And today, with all
their instruments, it is a pressing medical problem to determine when
death begins and when it is complete. Jesus showed that death *begins* in
the deathlike sleep of plenary trance—"our friend, Lazarus, sleepeth"—
and he showed that man can be returned to life from this state, in which
the body does not deteriorate. The "dead and buried" have been raised
from such trance. The mother of General Robert E. Lee is one example.
What principle is involved—why do some respond and others not?

The Stranger points to Scriptures which indicate that "in the last extremity of life, in death-trance, the ego-group of the patient will respond
only if the physical measure applied to the body is reduced in traumatic
impact to a *whisper* as the force penetrates the inward psychic reaches.
. . . Tyrrell describes the painful reemergence of a man from the hinter-
lands of life. . . . Jesus demonstrated that even from the extremity of
death it is possible to return a man's ego-group to its conscious existence,
but death processes were not arrested by Him when a person was beyond
the prime of life or when the body was not in good condition. . . . Of
the many called, few indeed respond. Perhaps in death one knows himself and is unwilling to return *to the condition of amnesia man calls
consciousness.*"

In the "illusory miracles," such as Jesus' walking across the water, he demonstrated that a person in trance will see and hear what the operator tells him to see and hear. The vision will be *real* to him, *but the miracle happens only to the percipient.* Strange, is it not, that the Gospel of St. Mark, which is considered to be the remembrances of Peter, does not report that Peter walked forth to meet Jesus.

In almost every case of visionary, illusory experience with Jesus there is difference in the way the episode is reported. Each account is subjective, given as that particular disciple experienced it. And there is evidence that everything was suddenly normal as the disciples were returned to their normal states of consciousness at a touch, by a word. Again, the pattern is that of being brought quickly out of trance.

Harold believed that Jesus created these symbolic dramas to reveal the psychological operation in the universe behind men's eyes. And that Jesus deliberately set up in the Gospels the contradictory reports so that these episodes must be questioned and studied until time revealed them to be demonstrations of the phenomena that can be produced while a subject is in trance. *But each demonstration also enfolded the pattern of some type of psychic operation. The Stranger* says:

> In the illusory miracles, Jesus created the symbolic dramas that portray man's experiencing the ultimate aspect of his being. These dramas are redrawn, or are seen piecemeal, in the descriptions many men give when commanding truth is aroused within them or when the intellect, like Peter, is sinking in the deeps of the mind. The illusory miracles portray psychic action in valid terms, and they give an insight larger than is possible in any attempt to describe what happens to the terrified visionary. If a man can grasp the Christ, as symbolized by Jesus, he will be able to withstand the psychic travail. When one is in the midst of the purgatorial ordeal, he cannot be helped by metaphysical dissertations and systems—a more "present help," a more human understanding, is required to meet his need: he must have something to turn to, a mental image of the Christ, a *symbol* of the grace of God in man, which will take him in hand, to which he may cling as a child. . . . Turning to prayer or to a religious symbol to still the inner tempest is likely only if one has had religious training as a child and prayer is a ritual with him. If, habitually, he turns away from violence, when he must suffer inner violence habit itself will stay the mind and hand from abuse of self or another.

Harold says that in the drama of the Transfiguration, Jesus indicated that at the height of realization "one is illuminated in his being and undergoes a metamorphosis which puts upon him the shining raiment of love." But as this happens, "the body and emotions he is 'roped to' will, like the disciples, be 'sore afraid.' " But if man has grasped the God-Son within himself, "this One will lead him up to the heights and safely down again—will warn him that the full meaning of this vision cannot be realized in life or so long as one is in this world, but he must none the less bear witness to it. The miracles upon the waters show that if a man is aware of the Christ in being, he may call upon this One to still the tempest in his mind, and that as he ventures out alone to meet truth upon the deeps, this One will stretch forth a hand to save him as he sinks."

The Christ in being—this One that *The Stranger* speaks of—is a person's own Authority-Ego, God-Son within him, to be seen as the *same* as Jesus portrayed in playing the role of *Son of man.*

"Lead us not into temptation . . ."

The Stranger says, "To know truth forever *tempts* the intellect; to know God or holiness forever *tempts* the intuition. Jesus saw that man's consciousness of God is revelation of God-being within him, saw that it is truth incarnate in him that *poses always the temptation to grasp and know it,* leading the mind to higher consciousness until fear engulfs. Jesus understood that such power as truth engenders must be shared to be had or tolerated in sanity. He saw that because each man is independent in his being, he will come to realize his independent existence and must struggle with this madness until he can grasp truth larger than his solitariness: the Fatherhood of God insuring the brotherhood of man, the Christ within himself as his indestructible bond with the whole of life insuring his communication and communion with each other human being, making him a free agent in a social whole wherein every person on earth has the *same* endowment of power, glory, and truth at his disposal when his conscious and *unconscious* domains are summed—the Beatitudes project this summation."

The Beatitudes are the "Blessed are the . . ." series that begin the Sermon on the Mount (Matt. 5:1-12), and *The Stranger* says that this discourse is itself a miracle because of the effect of Jesus' words upon succeeding generations. And in what Harold calls the "social miracles," Jesus showed that the power of suggestion moves groups of people to action and that man responds to truth when it is presented to him with shocking clarity:

> When Jesus entranced His audiences, He gave them the suggestion
> of sharing their hidden reserves of food, their hidden reserves of mercy,
> their hidden reserves of conviviality—and He gave them the suggestions

67

recorded in the Sermon on the Mount. The twentieth century, however, confronts a stark horror that is no less a miracle for its hue: Adolf Hitler entranced his audiences and loosed their "legion" along with his own upon a world that realizes it was somehow party to his acts. The drama of Legion shows the destructive potential arising from mass susceptibility which makes it possible to transfer manic Messianic impulses from one man to a large group.

In this drama, a maniac is asked to name his demon, and it calls itself "Legion," saying, "there is a host of us." Whereupon, Jesus casts Legion into a herd of swine that rush to their destruction in the sea. What does this strange demonstration teach?

The lessons to be learned from each miracle (and parable) are manifold. Harold says that the maniac, so the story goes, was chained but could not be kept bound. "Legion" represents a pattern of numerous repressed, subliminal fears bursting loose—a phobia that could not be defined or "named" because it consisted of a lifetime's accumulation of destructive emotions and "silent" small terrors which had grown into a powerful force that must by its very nature be sent somewhere. *The Stranger* says, "Jesus had revealed in a parable that a psychic force of destructive potential (an evil spirit) cannot be destroyed merely by driving it out of consciousness (repressing it) because it will return, its force increased, and devastate the 'house' from whence it came. In this parable and in the drama of Legion one may observe that as repressions are reversed and re-presented to consciousness, if they are not reconciled within it by a widened understanding they gather into a host of nameless, unrecognized fears, a mass that can no longer be dealt with one by one for they have lost their identity. The Authority-Ego must then present them to the world of self by casting their destructive force onto the cellular level, as symbolized by the swine. When transferred to or cast upon the animal flesh in which man is clothed, Legion drives it to panic and self-destruction. Thereby, Legion expends itself and the Authority-Ego wipes out an expression in flesh that can no longer contain its accumulation of unidentified fear. When Legion's tensions and conflicts cross over into the cellular realm, they give rise to a death-dealing disease which moves at panic's pace. . . . In society, man has had experience of one man, or one act, stemming the tide of panic—and certain individuals appear to be immune to panic's lure. Although man does not know how it is achieved, he does know that there is no panic-paced disease in which spontaneous remission has not taken place."

Each of us must contend with our own Legion—the accumulated fears and destructive emotions, the tensions and hatreds we have repressed. Since "panic-paced" and death-dealing diseases occur even in infancy, we must project that Legion may be carried over from a past life. Or it may accumulate into a host of prenatal or birth fears that destroy the chances of the individual to fulfill his life's promise. We know little or nothing of prenatal psychic influences.

The vast majority of us suffer the violence of Legion in our own flesh before our Legion becomes a host. Much of Legion is dispatched in small detachments that kick up no more than a common cold. We must remember, however, that fear is contagious. But so is laughter. And so are tears. So are a number of illnesses. Harold would say that you must remember to have your medical vaccinations because together with the physical protection they afford they also reduce the host of your Legion of fear, your concern that you might contract the disease.

The drama of Legion tells us that as we undergo life's physical, emotional, and mental stresses, a host of repressed fear is accumulated on the subliminal level. And it will be expressed in terms of mental illness if it reaches intolerable strength—else, it will be transferred to the cellular level, causing death-dealing disease. Since Legion must be expressed, we must learn to deal with it day by day so that it cannot mount its force, and is disposed of as nontraumatically as are the body's wastes. When we understand how to deal with our Legion, we will understand how to maintain our health.

Society must deal with its corporate Legion. *The Stranger* says, "Jesus saw that man may change only himself—that each man 'hath one' [his own Authority-Ego] which judges him and deals with his own evil and will in time save his own world. Society's salvation must follow. Society's Legion must be bound as the Lilliputians bound Gulliver. If a man can secure one cord upon it, he will find satisfaction: he may secure a cord upon it as he secures a cord upon his own. The man who thinks he can change society is expressing to some degree Messianic delusion. In the drama of Legion, Jesus showed that the attempt to rid man of evil in one grand play that changes society's dealing with him results in destruction of the masses. His whole ministry points to the realization that society cannot be delivered of its ancient evils within the life-span of any one man—not even upon the advent of a Messiah—for He tells of the struggles men will have to endure in society before the final struggle is met, and He indicates that this struggle will be met upon the psychic plane."

The Stranger is not saying that we should not try to right social wrongs—or that they cannot be righted. To the contrary. But progress in this direction *begins* with the individual's own behavior; and social problems must be handled one by one before they grow into an unidentifiable host that cannot be dealt with save in one grand play that defeats the purpose because of the traumatic effects it produces upon those who are "innocent" of the dilemma.

But here we are not dealing with social problems. We are dealing with psychic energy. The *unconscious* is the seat of the psychic power. Harold says that Jesus exercised His psychic power to show the real limits of this mysterious force in man, "so that any strange phenomenon that cannot be reconciled within the framework drawn by his deeds must be regarded with suspicion. . . . Jesus appears to have seen that the psychic power is deeply involved in awareness, perception, the process of learning, and artistic expression, so that to show its inward play upon man, and Himself to express the true limit of its power within and without oneself, was His mission. As teacher, He was artist and He used His psychic power to teach and demonstrate His lessons. In the lesson of the loaves . . ."

Here, we come to what Harold calls the "fantastic" miracles, which he believed were demonstrations of an operator's ability to obliterate the ability of his small audience to perceive what is happening. Perception is distorted. The opposite of hallucination occurs. "Hallucinatory blindness and deafness" is induced. A fantastic answer? Any good hypnotist with subjects in trance can produce this effect. And after a subject has been hypnotized to the desired state of trance, the operator can induce trance almost instantaneously by employing some unobtrusive signal.

The Stranger deals with the miracles *as they are reported*. The reports of the feeding of the multitudes do *not* say that Jesus commanded the few loaves and fishes to grow and that before the eyes of the people they grew as he broke them, nor that as the food was taken from the baskets more food appeared. The reports give only the beginning and the end of the drama. Because they tell nothing of what actually happened, Harold concluded that Jesus commanded his disciples in trance state to see everything *but where the food came from*. Expectancy played a role: "Jesus had the disciples arrange the people in groups. Each one was thus 'fixed' in the expectation of eating. Then He took what He had, gave thanks, broke the food into pieces and placed it before the crowd. The suggestion of sharing and eating, implemented by His own decisive action, must have spread with the lightning of telepathy throughout the crowd, for the simple story then ends, 'So the people ate and were satisfied.' . . . This event appears to be a spontaneous mass reaction to suggestion. . . ."

The disciples did not see that a perfectly natural thing was happening. People brought out their own hidden reserves of food, ate, and shared. The "miracle of the loaves" taught the lesson that the hidden reserves in man are sufficient to provide for life however hopeless the scene may appear.

Harold says that Jesus may have used this opportunity to teach another lesson: "a fantastic demonstration involving objective matter to a degree entirely beyond the creditable is not what it appears to be—through hypnosis, hallucination or hallucinatory-blindness has been induced. . . . Jesus said that faith as a grain of mustard seed could move a mountain, could uproot and transplant a tree in the sea. But *He made no such demonstration.* . . . In Jesus' words, a mustard seed is *as the realm of God*—this seed, less than any on earth, grows larger than any plant. Therefore, faith 'as a mustard seed' indicates *faith larger than is possible to Homo sapiens' consciousness* which cannot enfold the whole realm of God. . . . One might say, in truth, all things are possible, but the attempt to exercise faith that is potentially as great as the mustard seed Jesus described often flowers into fantastic hallucination, and what actually may be achieved through hypnosis is limited because there is a limit to the faith man can express, doubting not in his heart that what he asks will be done."

But Harold points out that Jesus said greater works would be done than he did, and that there are many demonstrations which have no explanation other than mental or psychic power affecting material substances. Nevertheless, of all psychic phenomena, psychokinesis (objects set in motion, affected, or produced through unseen means) is "least understood and is most likely to lead to self-deception and trickery if one embraces the concept too hastily."

There is one area, however, in which we *are* sure that an "unseen" force affects an object. That force is a person's own psychic energy; that object is his own flesh. We may also be reasonably sure that certain altered states of consciousness allow for *paranormal perception* giving the gifted subject commanding insight on the physical as well as the intellectual level. We know now that everything is surrounded by, permeated with, indeed, *is*, an energy field. We may expect to refine our sight or instruments—our receptors—to receive stimuli and information at levels undreamed of in Jesus' day, making possible and probable greater deeds than he performed. We know now that somehow the

Cosmic Mind generates from the ethereal "nothing" of these interpenetrating energy fields all the solid stuff there is.

We know today that mental or psychic energy can affect a growing plant. But Harold believed that the drama of Jesus' withering the fig tree was created to demonstrate posthypnotic response to suggestion—since one report says the tree withered instantly and another says it was seen to be withered next morning. The disciple who saw it withered next morning was responding to suggestion posthypnotically. But the episode was used to teach a deeper lesson: the power to produce an effect through the manipulation of an effigy. The drama also indicated that "the odious and irrational in life is best destroyed through a withering process that is initiated when one destroys a symbol representing whatever he would have done with."

This particular "miracle" embarrasses Christianity. It was not the time for the tree to bear its figs. Could God-Incarnate, Saviour of the world, essence of love itself, petulantly destroy a tree because it was growing normally?

The Stranger says, "An intricate message must be enfolded in this drama and it must hinge upon what the tree and its fruit represent. Jesus made a tree the symbol of Himself, calling Himself the vine. Thus, the withering of it becomes the withering of something to do with Himself. The incident takes place the morning after His entrance into Jerusalem, just before He is to provoke His own destruction in terms of an *effigy* of Judaic Messiah, on the cross. . . ." If the fig tree represented Jesus cast in the traditional Messianic role, which he sought to destroy, reversing the force of it by internalizing the concept, then his words, "may no one ever eat fruit from you after this," fall into place as the meaning behind this episode which *has* done so much to wither the concept of Jesus as God become flesh, to the exclusion of all other human beings. Now, listen to *The Stranger*:

> . . . the withering of the fig tree teaches that art is making an effigy of oneself to destroy through it the irrational or odious in life—to destroy it not explosively, but surely. At the same time the artist makes of his work a symbol to convey as large a measure of truth as he can. Thus, every artist is both destructive and creative. And every man is artist: of his life he creates both an effigy he would destroy and a symbol of truth he would express. As artist, Jesus was both destructive and creative—He destroyed the ancient Messianic mold and created the concept of the Christ in every man. Even the least bears this glory—is human, is divine. . . .

72

This "theater" of miracles has become as crowded as a ball park. Let the audience take a seventh-inning mental stretch. Then we will get on with a discussion of ESP.

S T R E T C H

"I'd like a bottle of beer and two hot dogs—lots of mustard."

"Where do you think you are?—in a ball park? Well, so we are. Hey you, with the beer! Over here, please."

> Jesus was called glutton and drunkard. He did not deny that He ate and drank as He chose— He stated that wisdom vindicates ascetic or non-ascetic practices: "For John the Baptist has come, eating no bread and drinking no wine, and you say, 'he has a devil'; the Son of man has come eating and drinking, and you say, 'Here is a glutton and a drunkard, a friend of taxgatherers and sinners!' Nevertheless, Wisdom is vindicated by all her children." Jesus provided wine at the wedding in Cana. Does His mysterious refusal of wine at the last supper provide the basis for a doctrine of abstinence—if so, making of Jesus a man reformed at the door of death? The teaching and practice of Jesus, however, do not invite to drunkenness or gluttony. He teaches that there is nothing in life that cannot be used to further its joy and abundance when man has learned to control himself. . . . He saw that men must grasp the art of play: "To what then shall I compare the men of this generation? What are they like? Like children sitting in the marketplace and calling to one another, 'We piped to you and you would not dance. . . .' "

"Another beer, and a hot dog for *The Stranger*."

"Is it true that laughter is made of every nastiness you can think of— aggression, sadism, and so on—like the psychologists say?"

"That's the way they've analyzed it. But what people will laugh at changes—almost from year to year."

Jesus did not laugh—did not smile so far as the record is concerned. . . . Jesus knew "what was in man." Thus, He would have known what prompts laughter, and the mystery of why He did not laugh is resolved. . . .

"He means that as symbol of a person's own Authority-Ego, Jesus could not represent it truly if it expressed hostility for its own world of consciousness, even through laughter, or humorously."

Although Jesus did not laugh, He offered that which has come to be identified with humor: salt. . . . "Salt is good. . . . Let there be 'salt between you' . . ." but let there be also humanity between men, for what good the salt if it has lost its savor? Jesus calls God love and good; He calls salt good; it must follow that aggression gentled through humor constitutes an essential ingredient of love, and that hostility will in time lose itself in laughter. . . . Jesus said, "everyone shall be salted with fire, and every sacrifice shall be salted with salt." These words give promise that man shall become immune to that which corrupts and that humor is playing a redeeming role in life. Jesus could not laugh; He could not risk that a fragment of the profound paradoxes He posed would be taken in jest. But the art of life—seen as an appreciative awareness and participation in it—was practiced by Him. . . . His was a total empathy, a compassionate rendering, an exquisite edition of the art of life.

"We seem to have a genius for making a lousy mess of life—those of us under and over thirty. What did *The Graduate* say?—emotional maturity in the average person arrives at about age twenty-nine and lasts for an hour or so?"[50]

"Like fools we rush in, and then where angels tread, we peter out. . . ."

If one calls his brother "fool," he has taken the first small step in judging life that leads to a

74

season in hell, to the rise of unconscionable fear
that engenders madness, else to judgment that
reborns his consciousness in the fire of pain that
is the blinding-seeing action. . . .

"The blinding-seeing action? What do you mean?"

In the agony that blinds one to the leprous in
himself and all others, a new face is born upon
him and upon each of his fellowmen—his every
contact with humanity is healed, his sanity or
inner world is saved.

"You mean he becomes blind to evil?"

"He means that we must not judge the world in terms of good and
evil—drawing lines. But what does the blinded man *see* that heals
his contacts? What does he understand?"

He has understood, finally, that the *human*, the
commonplace, is divine, that man can be neither
good nor evil—he can be sane or insane, and
sanity is more precious than life itself. In the
act of judgment, he grasps the grace of God,
understands it to be: *sanity*. He becomes a disciple of the Authority within him that revealed
unto him the hypocritical self-righteousness of
anyone who judges any other man, the world,
life, as evil. The act of judgment humbles him,
not before the world, but in his own heart.

"Who is the 'Authority' that judges him?"

Not Jesus, but a man's own "divine absence" is
his judge. Jesus says, "He that rejecteth me, and
receiveth not my words, hath one that judgeth
him: the word that I have spoken, the same shall
judge him. . . ." The Word, "I," the Logos in
man, is a definite sounding in an authoritative
voice that is one's own—and yet is apart from
any of one's selves. . . . It does not come from
consciousness, nor superego, nor ego-group—
these are in the sinking boat engulfed in fear—
nor does it lodge in consciousness, and thus it

cannot be captured in the personality world. One who has heard it knows it to be *sane*, to be the grace of God, given a man—his own of it—it is the "I" of himself lifted up, drawing his ego-group together into a communicable sanity in the ranks of Homo sapiens. . . . And afterwards, it is blessed to be an ordinary soul.

"Are you speaking of that old saw the preachers play upon—the 'fall' that is prompted by intellectual pride?"

Each man's experiencing of his own soul as he ventures upon the deeps of his being, each man's suffering the temptation of the intellect to explore the heights and depths of good and evil, leads to psychic travail that varies in degree from nebulous, mongering anxiety to the horrifying prospect of beholding madness in himself. No description of what happens can meet with general acceptance because the pattern of response to psychological stress and the symbols employed to describe it will vary.

"Could you suggest some of the forms it takes?"

The drama may not play itself out to any reportable conclusion; it may reach its end in agonizingly slow motion; it may be so confused one cannot remember it; it may happen spontaneously in a flash of realization that brings one through it with a sort of baptismal "gasp"—or it may come through the plodding of conscience in seemingly unrewarding labor, or through the wrestling of an intellect that will not "let go" until the "angel blesses." Conrad Aiken chose the word *Gehenna* to title his short piece, which describes the disintegration, the granularization, of one's soul as it struggles in the watery depths. . . .

"Gehenna—I associate that word with hell or *fire*—is hell the *watery depths?*"

In the world of spiritual perception, away from "solid land," the illusory miracles take place. In this world man becomes more than he was as he falls from the heights, sinks toward the abyss of madness, and through this ordeal grasps the hand of truth. The illusory miracles *show* the coming or awakening of the grace of God in man—this is the mystery, permeating every great religion, which cannot be explained. . . . A man with re-born consciousness turns again to the church. The petty, conditional requirements of dogma are passed over. . . . He simply knows himself to be involved in consciousness with the church and comes to it of his own accord—that which was irrational in it has somehow withered before his eyes—for through the ages it has borne the *symbology* that came to him as the grace of God in the midst of his private hell. . . .

"God! The idea of returning to the Church—dreary Sunday."

"He doesn't mean you have to go to Church. He means that you have to see the Church in its historical perspective—not bedamn it."

Jesus observed the Sabbath, but He disengaged the ritual day from its all-engulfing regulations, stating that the Sabbath is made for man . . . it is to be rewarding, rehabilitating—not monotonous —it is a habit man is to keep himself, for it breaks the chain of days however he lives and relieves him of the conscious or unconscious intensity that repetition or monotony mounts.

"What's so bad about intensity?"

Intensity grows as unobtrusively as Samson's hair, and will expend itself in violence. . . . Each person suffers to a greater or lesser degree his own violence be it reasonably or unreasonably aroused.

"Pardon me, I just arrived—can you tell me where *The Palestinian Mystery Play* is playing?"

77

Jesus sought the open beauty of mountains and sea, the solitude of far places. He came also to the cities, the marketplace, the feasts, and to the temple.

"*The Stranger* means, it is playing wherever you are playing. . . ."

"And what were you saying when I interrupted?"

"We were talking about intensity and self-judgment."

The Son in man is the Self-factor that will lead a person to reap in kind his sin and error. Thus, each punishes himself.

"Then there is no vicarious atonement."

"Vicariousness itself is the sin. If there were vicarious atonement our lives would be meaningless—we would also be living vicariously."

"Is there *no* atonement, no forgiveness?"

Jesus proclaims also that the power to forgive is vested in the Son, the Self-factor, and one's return on the bread he casts upon life's waters is hundred-fold. He saw that in reality a man cannot abuse a brother-being without in the same measure abusing himself; and that he cannot forgive a brother-being without forgiving himself a like measure of the evil he has done. . . .

"Hey! You with the beer—a bottle for the stranger. . . ."

"*The Stranger* has left—he has gone into the theater."

"The beer is for this young man who just joined us."

"My given name is I."

"What a coincidence! So is his, and so is mine."

"Everyone is going into the theater—come on, bring your beer."

"Where is the theater?"

"Right here in the world, where we are. Everyone has a reserved seat, or he wouldn't come in, you know."

"Just sit down."

"What a S T R E T C H that was. . . ."

"Listen, *The Stranger* is speaking."

> The name glorified in the thunderous moment
> sounding the voice from heaven appears to be
> "I" or "it"—in effect, "I am it," the Father's
> name each speaks, a glory now, to be glorified
> again as love transfigures man. In the Transfigur-
> ation, Jesus indicates that at the height of realiza-
> tion when one is illuminated in his being he
> undergoes a metamorphosis which puts upon
> him the shining raiment of love. . . .

"What a glorious bright night it is—here, 'by the sea, I and' . . ."

"I . . ."

"And I. I wish I had thought to get a box of popcorn."

"Take this wafer in your cupped hands . . . and place it upon your tongue."

"The body of Jesus?"

"If Jesus were here kneeling at the altar with you, he, too, would cup his hands—he too would take the wafer."

"Don't you see? There is a body of consciousness of which you partake. This is the meaning of the Eucharist."

"If you eat so much as a grain of wheat, you are partaking of the body of God, the flesh of God—there is no other body, no other flesh."

"Jesus made this clear by giving thanks every time he broke a piece of bread or ate a bite of food."

> The flesh any man wears in this world is the flesh
> of God, is God extended into living matter, and
> to live man must partake of that which is or has
> been living. . . . All that is enfolded in the Com-
> munion rite Jesus established cannot be elabo-
> rated at this point, but it may be pointed out
> that this rite dramatized the need of man to
> partake of the flesh and blood of brother-being

79

to come through this into life, for Jesus stated Himself a brother to mankind.

"What does he mean?"

"Hush, I cannot hear. . . ."

Only, however, as this food is handed him by his Authority-Ego, only as he has his being in the *unconscious* primarily, is this permissible—this is to say, as embryo, fetus, and infant. Thereafter, he must become as a child, must move forward from his parasitic state, reaching forth his own hand to partake of his share in nature's realm. . . .

"Thank you for the wafers and wine. Shall I say grace before I eat and drink?"

"Only if you give thanks not to Jesus, but with him."

"You do not pray to Jesus. You pray with him—Our Father."

"We should move closer—it's hard to hear on this mountaintop. . . ."

"But we are in our reserved seats!"

"There is always room for you when you are ready to move up front."

"Or closer to the center of your own being."

"I think we are talking to ourselves."

"Yes."

THE MIRACLE OF PERCEPTION

Harold saw that sensory stimuli alone cannot account for man's ability to perceive. "No description of events in the brain that is expressed in purely physical terms explains . . . what it is that bridges the gap between physical sensation and the perceptions in a man's consciousness." Therefore, he offered a theory that, insofar as his publishers are aware, has not been offered before, and it throws new light on the subject of extrasensory perception.

To Harold, sensory stimuli and extrasensory stimuli may be likened to two "liquid" strands of energy that meet in space-time and give rise to an "epoxylike" reaction, which in turn gives rise to the "solid" perception and comprehension that we call normal.

If any condition prohibits or diminishes sensory stimuli, the delicate balance is upset. Then abnormal, but not supranatural, perception occurs. Extrasensory stimuli come from the operation of a finer type of energy than the type we acknowledge to be physical. Therefore, they possess different properties and operate upon a different field. Electrical impulses are the most gross expression of universal energy—not the finest. Mental or psychic energy is still Cosmic energy. But it is another kind of expression of the parent energy that composes the Cosmos and all within it.

Harold saw that mental/psychic energy can be understood in terms of physical energy when physical energy itself is understood. This part of his work is discussed in *If Thine Eye Be Single* and *On the Nature of Universal Cross-Action*.

Extrasensory stimuli impinge upon us constantly, and we assimilate much more information than we are consciously aware of—just as we assimilate much more sensory stimuli than we are aware of. And just as in outer space the sun is below the horizon and into tomorrow before we see it setting, so our inner light is always ahead of consciousness's sight.

Jesus appears to have seen that *man's insight* is the greatest miracle nature has wrought. Insight enfolds the past (postcognition) and shows the future possibilities (precognition) inherent in the situation. This allows man to see through the whole arrangement and to perceive what he must do. Insight allows man to pose himself a problem and solve it. The more "abstract" the problem he poses, the closer the answer touches upon underlying reality.

The problem confronting Jesus was how to conclude his drama in such a way that:

1) He would be a true symbol of *light*.
2) He would be a true symbol of a person's Authority-Ego.
3) He would fulfill prophecy regarding Messiah, thereby sealing his claim to the role that would be finished and destroyed in his person.
4) *And* in solving his problem he must act with *the integrity* that marked his course from beginning to end.

The Stranger's Solution to the Mystery of the Resurrection

The Palestinian mystery play has revolved for the past two thousand years around the Death and Resurrection of Jesus. There has been much speculation about what really happened, including the suggestion that the Crucifixion drama was nothing more than a "plot" through which it could be made to appear that Jesus had died and come back to life in order to gain support for his Messiahship. Such an idea, of course, destroys the integrity of Jesus and those who supposedly plotted with him in the scheme that failed because he died later of the spear wound and was secretly buried. No kind words about Jesus would, in such circumstances, erase the implication that his whole ministry and message was involved in a grand hoax that did not come off.

Harold did not believe that there was a "plot." To begin with, the prophecy that Messiah must fulfill was not a demand that the body of the One to come must be roused from death and resume its normal functions. The prophecy said that the body, the flesh, of this One would not *suffer decay in the grave*. The necessity, then, was to demonstrate control of the flesh by psychic power exercised in the death process in such a way that desiccation of the flesh would not occur.

Harold believed that the legends of Moses' and Elijah's strange *disappearance* indicated to Jesus that the utmost exertion of psychic power to bring about a psychosomatic reaction would induce an "internal cremation," which would cause his body to "vanish" into a handful of dust. We know that organic changes can be effected under hypnosis and that extraordinary physical reactions have been demonstrated. The question becomes—to what degree can exertion of psychic power affect the flesh?

The Stranger offers the conjecture that as Jesus passed from life into the state of death, he uttered the cry (of certain pitch) that would initiate posthypnotic organic response to autosuggestion made in advance, *causing a rapid disintegration of his flesh into dust—the end nature slowly accomplishes*. Jesus, as symbol of Adam, man, become fully conscious of himself as offspring of Cosmic Parent-Being, must like Adam return to dust. God-consciousness had said to Adam, "dust thou art, and unto dust shalt thou return."[51]

Harold points out that Jesus spoke of casting fire on "earth" and of a strange "baptism" he must undergo; and of the tension he must suffer until this be accomplished. Casting fire on earth—the "earth" of his own flesh? Baptismal—in that he could not test his conviction that through exercise of psychic power he could quickly reduce his body to earth, dust? What could "casting fire" mean?

As illumination comes, many men describe it as an inward conflagration. Richard Maurice Bucke described the moment as coming when he was in a quiet and passive state (which means that he was in a degree of trance). Without warning, he felt as though he were enveloped in a flame-colored cloud and thought of fire, but realized that the flame was within. Understanding came as in a flash of lightning.[52] Such illumination may be an expression in smallest degree of the inward flame that in *the greatest degree of its expression* can effect "internal cremation."

In order to fulfill Messianic prophecy, Jesus must accomplish something else. He must die quickly enough that not a bone of him would be broken. Harold believed Jesus knew that fear can *kill quickly* by bringing on a state that today physicians would call "shock." This type of shock often causes death when the physical injuries a person has sustained would not. The blood separates into a colorless serum and a heavy mass.

The Stranger says Jesus knew how to open the door of his inner realm and let a host of fear—his Legion—cast itself upon his body, knowing that it would rush him to death, just as the Legion cast into the swine caused them to rush to destruction. In the cry, "My God, my God, why hast thou forsaken me,"[53] Jesus indicated that he let fear flood his body on the Cross, and death came quickly. The record says that when the spear struck, blood and "water" (serum) came from Jesus' side.[54] Today, we can see that fear, bringing on the state of shock, was the killer. In his medical ministry, Jesus had shown over and over that fear tends to kill and faith tends to restore to health. Almost always, he began his healings with, "fear not," and ended with, "your faith has made you whole."

Jesus' cry, "My God, my God, why hast thou forsaken me," also showed the pattern of the culmination of the Messianic complex: unconscionable fear overcomes the sufferer at the height of his realization. Jesus on the Cross, "King of the Jews" written above his head, was the *effigy* of Messianic delusion which, at the end, he had let be created of himself in order to lead the ancient Messianic tradition to destruction in his person.

But neither fear nor the necessity to reveal the pattern of Messianic delusion had the last word on the Cross. As the ordeal was finished, Jesus—magnificent human being that he was—said, "Father, into thy hands I commend my spirit." Faith triumphed. And Jesus' spirit—his psychic energy—began accomplishing its task of reducing his body to dust.

We have said before that in his interpretation of Jesus, Harold calls upon only natural phenomena, which are demonstrable and are supported by a body of evidence. Harold acknowledged that in suggesting disposal of Jesus' body through "internal cremation," he had departed from this ground. He offered this solution only as a conjecture, and pointed out that there are other answers which fit into the pattern of posthypnotic response to suggestion. Jesus could have roused himself from deathlike trance. But if he did, the Gospel records clearly show that *he did not appear in the flesh to his followers.* Therefore, Harold concludes that Jesus then acted to fulfill prophecy by disposing of his body in a way that it *would not see decay in the grave*, which was the requirement, and true to his word gave his life to seal his mission.

The Stranger shows that *by Jesus' own words, his Resurrection was not to be literal. He said that the world would see him no more—thereby indicating that he would not again appear in the flesh in normal ways.*

Having said that the world would see him no more, Jesus then described to his disciples the visionary nature of his reappearance to them. He speaks of appearing *only* to those who possess his commands and love him. He says that on that day he will be living in *another realm*, "in my Father." But he will also be living in his disciples' inner realms, as they will live on in his. The image and knowledge, each of the other, is a living reality in the ongoing world of each.[55]

The very end of the Gospel of St. Mark, which is acknowledged to be the earliest one and is considered to be the "bone structure" of Jesus' record, is lost. There is very little in it about the Resurrection. But *all* the reports we do have in this and other Gospels clearly imply that Jesus' appearances to his disciples after the Crucifixion were visionary. The reports indicate that these visions merged quickly into the reality that attaches to hallucinations. But *The Stranger* says that regardless of the reality these experiences assumed, once the vision appeared, in each case it is clearly indicated that the encounters were abnormal, first and last. In the visionary encounters, the words, Jesus *had* spoken, the commands he *had* given, came to those who possessed them already, because they had been implanted in their minds previously.[56]

It was necessary for Jesus to conclude his drama by disposing of his body and not appearing in the flesh in order to complete his revelation of the power of psychic energy over the body and to show the psychic dynamics of contact with the dead in a valid way. Jesus must show that after death a person can return to those left behind only in a subjective way, as the still living image of the dead one in their minds rises to their consciousness and communicates with them as realistically as though the dead one himself were there. He must show that the dead live on as an integral part of the life of each person who has known them. This is true also of those who are or have become literary figures, as Jesus is today, and as Moses and Elijah were in Jesus' day.

The Gospel records show that Jesus made no secret of implanting in his disciples' minds the *suggestion* that they would see him on the third day after his death. The Resurrection drama shows the pattern of post-hypnotic response to suggestion.

Indeed, Jesus' whole drama is a revelation of the operation of psychic energy in man. It is a revelation of man's natural power designed to show the valid limits of its expression as well as the *delusions that can be engendered when this power is not understood.* Jesus set up the contradictions in the reports of the miracles that would force examination of them until their true nature was comprehended. There were no words then to describe the mysterious phenomena of hypnosis—the "mysteries" that had held mankind in bondage to superstition and fear, inviting the practice of dark magic.

Jesus explained as clearly as it was possible then to explain in words that after his death he could show himself *as he was in life* only in the *minds* of living men who knew him and in whom he had implanted the suggestion that they would see him; or that his presence could be felt as any man was transformed in the mind of the beholder into Jesus' essence-in-being as the stranger's face took on the compassionate look that Jesus must have worn, vesting his eyes with the *look of the Christ,* which can rise to the eyes of any person.

In the Resurrection drama, Jesus showed that there are two ways in which communication between the dead and the living can take place. First, actual information (verbalized) which comes from the dead has been implanted in the minds of those who received it while the dead one was still living. The recipient is not always aware of the knowledge. It may have been received by telepathy and stored in the subconscious without making appearance in consciousness, so it appears to be new information. The "materializations" accompanying such revelations are hallucinations which are so easy to induce that the person experiencing them does not realize this and has no idea that he has been led into trance state. In this state, a person's own extrasensory perception is heightened. *The hallucinations seem so real because ESP is an essential part of normal perception.* Psychic, sensory, and mental force is needed to "compose" whatever scene we ever see, or whatever sound we ever hear, and the power to hallucinate is involved in everything we perceive.

Jesus also showed that the dead who are living on another plane—in the realm of their *unconscious*—can communicate with the living, but only through or upon this plane of being in the living person. Contact is on the *unconscious* level. At this level, communication is so complete, so full of meaning, that it cannot be verbalized and conveyed as information in the ordinary sense of the word. What comes is understanding, perfect in its wholeness, enveloping the total being of the recipient. The totality of the experience so energizes him that his reaction is physical, emotional, mental. It is a reaction such as a *dream* can produce when it brings one out of sleep and into a waking vision. Communication with the dead is structured through a dream or dreamlike state. It is impossible to describe the *synthesis* of all that has been imparted. After Jesus' death, the disciples must have experienced such total communication with his still living psyche. In the Gospel of St. Luke (24:45), it is described as Jesus' *"opening their understanding"* that they might understand the Scriptures.

Contact with the still-living dead, which comes as communication on the *unconscious* level, may also take the form of inclination to do something that leads one into a situation so poetic or so meaningful that it brings to consciousness a message that is real. The message is real because what is *felt* in the dramatic moment is consistent with the totality of the experience the two people have had together and with all that such experience could project. This, too, is more than can be put into words. The experience is completely subjective and therefore is not susceptible of proof or verifiable demonstration.

The dead cannot explain in words that the living can understand what it is like to be on the other side of the veil. Communication can take the form only of a feeling of assurance that life and love continue.

The Resurrection drama shows that communication with the living dead is a *direct* one-to-one correspondence between those involved. Such correspondence neither requires nor permits the intervention of mediums on either side of the veil. All a medium can do is read what has been implanted in the mind of another. Feelings of guilt, remorse, ambivalence, may call up images and remembrances from the subconscious, and these may haunt one's dreams. But this, too, is self-contained communication—not real contact.

Jesus' words say that actual communication comes only as love calls and love answers. If love is real, honest, it will lead the communicants to release each other and be content with remembrance and the promise of a tomorrow. If love is not real, honest, neither will the communication be real, although communication with self-contained knowledge may go on for as long as a person wishes to indulge it. And because man's power to hallucinate is real, he may conjure up as often as he will materializations born of his own imagination.

Jesus did not mislead anyone. Mankind is prone, even determined, to mislead itself. The visionary appearances of Jesus had greater impact because his body was not in his tomb. Only the linen cloth in which he had been wrapped was there—shielding a handful of dust?

Jesus made it clear that the coming of the *Son of man*, which *all* who were present with him or living in his time would see, is an *inward* event that must take place for each individual at his death. But we cannot escape the fact that Jesus also implied that *he* would come back. We do not need to try to escape this implication.

The Stranger says Jesus *did* come back into the world, and within the lifetime of the beloved disciple. But he came back in precisely the same way as he had told the world that each one of us comes back: the Father raises the dead and makes them live, *ye must be born again*. In an hour his disciples expected not, in a way unrecognizable even to himself, Jesus was born again and died again—soon, *The Stranger* says.[57] Why? Because Jesus did not need to live long. His empathy for life in Homo sapiens' generation was complete, and he was ready to enter life in a more mature species. Perhaps in another of the Father's many mansions?

There is one more mystery connected with the Crucifixion and Resurrection drama—a mystery that haunts the conscience of Christianity. Judas, the betrayer. Christianity hangs itself in making Judas the culprit who must bear the blame for Jesus' death. One wonders how many more years will pass before Judas is officially "exonerated."

Harold shows, using Jesus' own words, that Judas was instructed and commanded to his act by Jesus.[58] And that Judas was his trusted friend, the only one Jesus could count on to perform the awful role that was an absolute necessity to the drama of *light*, which Jesus also symbolized —inner and outer light.

In the drama of light, there must be opposing wave trains of action, operating on different frequencies, which reinforce each other at the central point, thereby *providing a boundary for light's action*. This effect is known as "constructive interference." Judas played the "opposing role," providing "constructive interference."

The Judas role was also necessary to show that in accordance with the operation of nature's supreme law, the second law of thermodynamics, a measure of energy (heat) is *lost* as each cycle of action completes itself. Jesus speaks of having to lose *one*. New energy must be supplied if the action is to continue—St. Paul fills this role.

And, in order to fulfill Messianic prophecy, the potter's field must be purchased. Judas purchased it.

And, if Jesus' revelation of the culmination of the Messianic complex was to be complete, he must show that the "betrayed" *arranges for his own betrayal—insists upon it*.

Jesus did not misuse Judas. Each of his disciples was committed to giving his life if need be to help him in his work. Judas understood, but dimly, the nature of the role he must play. When the time came, he faltered—but did not fail. He somehow understood that truth, guiding the drama from the *unconscious* realm, insisted upon fulfillment of the awful role because through the Jesus–Judas drama the mystery of good and evil *that act together* is highlighted.

When he had finished his mission, Judas committed an act that he was not commanded to by Jesus, although Jesus had forewarned him of the horror that would overtake him. Judas did a very *human* thing. Unable to live with his agony, he killed himself.

And so, as happens in the drama of light's propagation, the opposing wave trains "cancel out" in phase—together.

But before we move on to a discussion of good and evil, we must say a word to those who may resent or be disturbed by Harold's putting the spotlight on Jesus' words, which clearly state that his Resurrection would not occur in the literal sense, but it would occur as a psychic—a spiritual —event *to those who loved him and possessed his commands*.

We would say that spiritual, psychic happenings are *real*. Unless we can accept this simple fact, there is no ground upon which religion of any sort can stand—no footing for psychology, no explanation of a reborn consciousness, or for psychosomatic phenomena that confront physicians every day. Jesus' Resurrection is no less real for its being visionary experience and communication with his still living being on the *unconscious* level from whence dreams bring their strange cargo of truths.

Today, when numbers of those who appear to be "clinically dead" have been returned to life, what meaning does a resurrection of Jesus in the flesh have? We cannot concede that our modern resurrected people were actually dead—the actually dead do not come alive again in the same flesh. If Jesus returned in the body that suffered on the Cross, then he did not actually die on the Cross.

Therefore, there is but one reality upon which the Resurrection of Jesus can rest—a psychic event, *real*, and so seminal in meaning for those who experienced it that the truth Jesus revealed in these few days rings through the centuries with the only promise regarding the hereafter that he ever made: each life is everlasting, our own inner world without end. Amen.

And when, in time, through the many lives we live, our consciousness becomes complete and incorruptible, this consciousness will express flesh that is complete and incorruptible—a body that death no longer need divest us of.

SCENE VII

The Mystery of Good and Evil

"Before you get going again, may I ask if it would be evil for me to bring sex into the dialogue?"

"Who considered it a sin in the first place?"

> *St. Paul, not Jesus,* beclouded the subject of sex with sin, or saw it as immoral, an evil of the flesh that man must contend with.

Suppose we let Harold speak directly to the question.[59] He says, "When one gathers Jesus' words on the subject of sex, he sees that Jesus expressed a very different attitude toward sexuality from that expressed by St. Paul. In answer to the Pharisee's question of divorce, He refers to Scripture that attests to the need, right, and desirability of male and female to engage in sexual union. . . . Because God, Love, joins them, male and female are not to be put asunder—thus, in Jesus' view it is not an 'excellent thing to have no intercourse with a woman,' " as St. Paul puts it, consenting to marriage only because "there is so much immorality, that every man had better have a wife of his own and every woman a husband of her own."

Jesus said to his questioner, "Have ye not read, that he which made them at the beginning made them male and female, and said, for this cause shall a man leave father and mother, and shall cleave to his wife: and they twain shall be one flesh?" Here, he turns us to think upon the beginning of man and woman, their innate equality, their needs as individuals and in their male and female roles. *The Stranger* says:

> . . . each person is as Adam: a body of consciousness through which is expressed a body of his own that he takes to wife, for Adam is joined to his *own flesh* in Eve. Thus man cannot separate himself from the desire for a body, or from the desires of his body, on the assumption that life

90

can be divorced from physical manifestation and the need of male and female in Homo sapiens generation to express their sexuality. But Jesus' listeners did not grasp the poetry of the Adam-Eve legend: humankind wedded each to himself in the beginning, and then each sex to the other. Nor would they accept His presentation of the equality of the sexes, so they replied, "Better not marry at all!" Jesus answers this plaint, "True, but this truth is not practicable for everyone, it is only for those who have the gift." These words do not prohibit the indulgence of sexual desire. To the contrary, they are utterly permissive. But they are also practical, for few have the gift to live and love freely. Jesus then lifts the discussion to another level: continence. He says that men are born eunuch, are made eunuch, or make eunuch of themselves for the sake of the realm of heaven, which is to say, in response to inner need. Such continence is to be practiced only if practicable.

Jesus saw that man's nature is changing. In time he will not need the bonds marriage imposes to make him behave responsibly toward the other sex and the children that derive from the union. He saw also that the inner worlds of two people cannot be fused to become "one world," so that any consorting with another in thought or deed adulterates one's inner world in the sense that it brings to bear upon self-union. Harold says:

> Homo sapiens therefore represents an adulterous generation, and is dissatisfied because the Self of himself for which each person searches cannot be found in another, nor in the personality one exposes, nor in the frailty he knows his consciousness to be. Nor can the longing for this Self-absence be mitigated more than temporarily by loving or lusty union with another.

Jesus did not say that divorce should be prohibited—he pointed out that Moses had given a "bill of divorcement" upon which mankind could call, but he indicated that it was not equitable and did not touch upon the reality of the situation. Harold says:

> In Jesus' encounter with the Samarian woman at the well, He shows that in Homo sapiens' inner world he can never be divorced from any part of his experience with another, for He numbers the men she has known, indicating that the image of every person with whom one has become one flesh lives with him as consort in his kingdom within. In the psychic sense, then, divorce is an illusion. And one cannot be divorced by law from whatever problem it is within himself that causes his marriage to become mean bondage or contributes to its failure. Jesus' emphasis on words must lead one to strive to master the problem with the person he has wed in his vow before God and man, for this vow

broken divorces him from his word as his bond, creating in his human power a dichotomy he must live with.

Here, we may pause to consider the nature of the marriage vow imposed upon so many well-meaning souls. To put it mildly, it does not reflect the teaching of Jesus. To tell the truth, it ought to be against the law.

"What God hath joined together . . ."—consider what "God" means, as described by Jesus. God is spirit, good, love. Spirit means psychic energy, operating above and below consciousness or on another frequency that cannot always be described in rational terms. Good is that which brings true satisfaction, "salt," humor, empathy for the other. And love must engender delight in life, though with it comes the *agonia*—the pain of loving, which is also the measure of its joy.

As long as any one or all of these measures are binding, a union is a union. But when any one or all of them cease to function, there is, actually, no union to be "put asunder." A state of unhappy legal bondage exists.

As long as God binds a union, the partners cherish and support each other. When God ceases to bind the union, the marriage vows cannot in truth be kept. As for "forsaking all others," how many can escape adultery? Harold says, "Jesus named adultery for what it is—lust. 'I tell you, anyone who even looks with lust at a woman has committed adultery with her already in his heart.'" And what is sauce for the gander is also sauce for the goose.

Marriage vows predestine the partners to break their word, to greater or lesser degree. And each time one's *word* is broken, having been solemnly given, confidence in himself decreases—although he may not be aware of this or admit it.

Marriage begins whenever God brings two people into union. Marriage vows should reflect this union and commit the partners only to act responsibly and equitably toward each other and their children, whatever the course their lives take thereafter. No vow should be taken, "until death do us part"—because life can also engender a parting of the ways that may well be for the good of all concerned.

Jesus saw the necessity, the practicality, of making marriage a legal estate that tends to enforce responsible action upon the participants. He recognized also that there are intolerable marriages, so that society needs a bill of divorcement to dissolve these. But in his day, and in our day, neither the marriage vows nor the bills of divorcement reflect the true nature and need of mankind. Harold says:

Jesus commanded humankind to love one another in every sense of the word, for love joined them in the beginning in sexual union and this He pointed out. He saw bondage of any sort, however, to be hateful—be it bondage to lust's insatiable appetite, or bondage to ignorance, or to illness, or to a religious priesthood's sometimes greedy and sometimes ridiculous demands. Jesus spoke truth to free man—not to bind him to social laws that fail to reflect the truth of his nature and of the situation with which they attempt to deal. He spoke truth to free man from his own self-deceptions that lead him to circumvent social law even as he transgresses psychic law, for these transgressions take a heavier toll of him. He spoke truth to free mankind of degrading traditions that cripple the soul of male or female.

Sexual expression in itself is not the sin—degrading oneself or another is. This is the point Jesus makes whenever sexual intercourse of any sort, inside or outside the bonds of marriage, enters the picture. Harold says, "He neither condemns nor condones the rescued adulteress: 'Neither do I condemn thee: go, and sin no more.' Nor does He scorn the sinning woman, bathing His feet with her tears. He says that one who has much love will be forgiven much, and one who has not much to be forgiven, has not much love."

Let those of us who have much to be forgiven thank God, thank love for its forgiving nature. And let us remember that sexual intercourse is the means through which life's new and triumphant generation has been brought forth. So, with love, and with Jesus, we give it our blessing.

We may digress here to say that although life is now sexually based, Harold accepted the virgin birth of Jesus, and many others in human history. He pointed out that parthenogenesis (development of embryo from unfertilized egg) may possibly be accomplished unconsciously— just as false pregnancy is a psychosomatic phenomenon. Although so far scientists have produced in their laboratories only female offspring via parthenogenesis, at some point nature must have produced the first male cell through some type of cross-action between female cells. In rare cases, the primordial pattern repeats itself and a male child is produced through unconsciously accomplished parthenogenesis.[60] A man (or woman) born of a virgin may be thought of as clothed in the flesh of "primordial maleness."

Remember, please, that Adam and Eve are of the same generation— man and woman of "one flesh" vested with Son-consciousness. Therefore, we cannot see the one as good (positive) and the other as evil (negative)—if we hold the idea that the "negative" label is derogatory.

Actually, as we shall see, expression of the negative is as essential to life as expression of the positive—good and evil must operate together in the natural realm.

*   *   *   *   *

The secret of good and evil—as Harold saw it and believed that Jesus saw it—is: in its *maximum* expression, good turns into evil; in its *minimum* expression, evil turns into good.

Good and evil act in concert—always. God (good) and the serpent (evil) in Eden "program" the course of man. The Jesus–Judas drama lays down this pattern. Good (positive energy) and evil (negative energy) operate harmoniously throughout nature—the one is as necessary to the other as the electron is to the proton.

Good's expression gives rise to *constructive potential*—but life can no more tolerate the maximum expression of constructive potential than the body can tolerate the uncontrolled construction of cells that cancer generates.

Evil's expression gives rise to *destructive potential*—it is the disorganizing force. If it were not for the operation of a disorganizing force, life and creation could be "finished" or completed. Because of the operation of the destructive potential, hand in glove with the constructive potential, life cannot be finished, and creation cannot be completed. Therefore, life is everlasting and creation continues *ad infinitum*.

Evolution is the process of disorganizing and reorganizing the potentials of good and evil until the *optimum* expression of each potential is reached. All things work together for the good—so we are told. Nature is such a constructor! Such an organizer! Will good totally overcome us? Take heart. Jesus says, "Sufficient unto the day is the evil thereof" (Matt. 6:34).

As most scientists interpret nature's supreme law—the second law of thermodynamics—nature is not busily constructing and organizing. To the contrary. This law is interpreted to mean that fuel to heat the universe is constantly being disorganized, and there is nothing to indicate that it is being organized anew. There is an always increasing measure of the random element, and this measure is called entropy. The increase of entropy leads to the decrease of temperature. Hence, these scientists predict the "heat death" of the universe. Harold disagreed. He insisted that entropy must be treated as a *signed number*, and that the apparent effect is always balanced by a like measure of opposite effect, which is unapparent, so that disorganization and organization are maintained in desirable balance as reorganization continues.

To say that nature's supreme law has but one meaning or aspect, destructive in nature and promise, is to say that evil (negative potential) can operate apart from good (positive potential) of a constructive nature and promise. It is also to say that the *absolute* can be expressed and that the *absolute state* can be achieved. Nothing in empirical data or observation supports this conclusion.

At the maximum, both good and evil attempt to express absolute power. But *expression of the absolute* was finished in life and in the universe in the devolution of God that *was*, which coincides with the beginning of evolution. The absolute state changed from "expression" into a state of "being." God is. The Cosmos is. Within this being, absolute expression of any sort is prohibited by the operation of the supreme law, which takes its toll of every expression of power, and tithes the energy, banking it in space, providing a reserve for tomorrow.

We must understand that, because the absolute cannot be expressed, *every* act in nature, and by man, involves the expression of good and evil. Positive and negative potentials are inherent in it; constructive and destructive potential is spent; and the results of the act will involve some measure of both forces.

Man and nature are being "delivered" from evil's destructive power by expending and experiencing it. Through this process evil's potential is reorganized and constantly reduced. In time, and through experience, man must so attenuate his ability to do evil that its residual expression turns it into good.

We must understand that to attempt to separate completely good and evil in life and to express evil so absolutely as to have done with it or rid the world of it in one grand play is to do such evil deeds as only *insanity* can engender. When man attempts to overresist or to overdo good or evil, he runs into trouble. He deludes himself if he thinks he does only good—or evil. A measure of each will be operative, just as in the atom the proton and electron are both involved in the play.

Whenever we attempt to express maximum good, good turns into evil, as it inevitably does when man attempts to "play God," or be "the absolute" in any endeavor. Who can call himself good? Jesus said, "Why callest thou me good? There is none good but one, that is, God. . . ."[61] God, the positive and absolute existence of space, the Cosmos, remains; but the play of energy has been given over to nature (mammon) and man in which good and evil are met.

Life is "weighted" toward the positive, the constructive. We see this in the mass of the proton versus the exquisite wisp of energy that the electron is. But we must remember that the proton can express in negative terms, as antiproton; and the electron can express in positive terms, as positron. *The Stranger* says:

> The fruit of the tree of life that would give man imperishable flesh could not be partaken of, after knowledge of good and evil had been incorporated in his consciousness and being, until life had taught him the secret of these opposing forces and had attenuated through many generations the *virulence of both*. . . . Up through the strange, twisted tree of knowledge that turns good to evil, and evil to good, man must grow, led by the spirit of attraction first to the one idea and then to the other, to become neither good nor evil, but divinely human—as love is.[62]

"Tell us, *why* must sin enter life—and how original is it?"

Each person is initially endowed with one full measure of the absolute power of God that *was*. Each one's measure of good and evil (or constructive and destructive potential) is no more, no less, than any other's. Sin enters life because the potential for evil-doing is inherent in total power, in God-power, with which man is endowed.

"Original sin" can come to rest only upon the doorstep of the "Absolute Parent Energy and Mind," which endowed man with its power as it cast its substance into its creation. Man can sin against himself or fellowman—but he cannot sin against God. The idea of sinning against God is, indeed, a foolish notion. As man shares in God-power, total, he must share also in the "sin" that is inherent even in the minimum and divided measure of such power that a person represents, a God-given measure of it. *Self*-judgment has been given into each one expression of this power. God cannot be sinned against, and God does not judge. Man can be sinned against, and each man judges himself—although he may not be aware of this.

Each of us lives only once in the body we inhabit. No one owns "for keeps" the flesh his consciousness generates. This material body is a temple of God's *pure evil*, or matter, because *evil* is the symbolic word for matter. Upon this body made of God's flesh the destructive expressions in life are cast. Thereby, man's evil is expiated in the destruction of the "flesh of God," which his own body *is*.

In each lifetime, man earns at least a modicum of understanding, which is the currency he needs to purchase, from the Cosmic store, matter of his very own—a body he can keep when he has learned how not to corrupt it and how not to corrupt the society of man and nature in which life has its being. Death must be built into life until man's understanding is complete.

"Scripture says that the sins of the father are visited upon the child. If God is father, then God's sin must be visited upon us?"

"Blasphemy! Isn't it?"

"An illogical conclusion, logically arrived at, I would say! Or vice versa."

As we share in the glory, grace, and reality of life, we must also share in its sin.

Judas symbolizes the sin that each man brings to life and knows not what it is. Its wage is death. But through paying this wage, man's evil is redeemed.

The "Judas-sin" represents something a person has done for which he has been unable to forgive himself in a past life. Or, it is knowledge that he cannot bear to live with forever, and as the sin is committed, it is repressed. It enters the newborn world of consciousness unknown, even to itself. It is derelict, nameless, and an outcast in the world of the ego-group. Only through death can this knowledge be buried in the "potter's field" of our personal worlds, which each of us purchases with blood money, as Judas did. What is deposited there is not remembered. Death, then namelessness in life, and then death again stand between us and that which we would cast out of our lives. Just as in the "potter's field" time turns derelict substance into pure matter, so in the "potter's field" of consciousness our evil is recast and purified.

As this nameless evil is abstracted from consciousness through the death process and is cast into the "psychic random element" under the control of good's "adverse chance," our psychic energy suffers a measure of disorganization and the potential for evil-doing is lessened. In the lessening of evil's potential for destructive action, there is an automatic shift in balance between man's forces. This produces an increase in his potential for constructive action in relation to the prior arrangement of his powers. Destructive potential can culminate only as it moves "hand in hand" with a like measure of constructive potential. In the outer world, in our age, the possibilities inherent in atomic power represent this psychic parallel.

The force of good (positive) and of evil (negative) energy is expended in every act, and in every act psychic energy is disorganized and recast into a measure of psychic force that is beyond either good or evil. We call this psychic force *empathy*. It is the measure of our humanity, the mark of the divine in man.

The Diminishing Role of Sin and
the Growing Role of Empathy

Empathy expresses the constructive potential born of understanding. Empathy derives from knowing in our very depths the whole measure (the good and the evil) of the situation that confronts us and the feelings of all involved. Empathy prevents a person's doing unto another what he would not have done to himself, because the empathetic soul suffers in his own being the pain that comes to another and the pain that he beholds. As empathy increases, evil-doing decreases. As we undergo the various experiences in the many lives we lead, the measure of our empathy—our *understanding*—constantly increases, so that the measure of empathy at work in society constantly increases. And empathy demands progress in the expression of humanity between individuals in society. Progress in mankind's expression of humanity between men is moral progress. Ideas of morality change from generation to generation—but the expression of true humanity between men and in society remains the basic measure of morality in any time or clime.

In the psychic realm, evil is organized as *raw lust*, and each person is endowed with one full measure of it. As this "fuel" is consumed, it produces as side product (and often as end product) the "psychic heat" of greed, covetousness, anger, and untempered fear that leads to abusive behavior in one way or another. But, as lust is expressed, its forces are disorganized, its powers are weakened. At "lowered temperature" and in attenuated form, lust's expression transmutes into the expression of humor, wit, laughter, ingenuity, idea, desire for life and love—into all that makes life worth living.

The decrease of lust spells the increase of compassion—of empathy. Empathy does not lead to the death of desire or the cessation of passion. To the contrary, the empathetic condition so enormously enhances life that the measure of a person's empathy is the measure of his capacity to enjoy it.

Harold was among the first to say that the constantly increasing empathy in the psychic realm parallels in the material realm the operation of nature's supreme law, through which there is a constant increase of entropy.[63]

Just as disorganization of lust in the psychic realm leads to organization of empathy (the constructive psychic potential), so in nature the organization of energy into usable fuel keeps pace with the disorganization of the fuel that is consumed. Harold outlined the dynamics of this process in his hypothesis, *On the Nature of Universal Cross-Action*. In his view, a perfect but ever-changing balance is maintained through the process of evolution in the physical and psychical realms that leads toward expression of the optimum rate of change and changing arrangement of opposite forces to allow for the constant renewal of all that is needed to sustain life and the desire for it.

Harold saw that nature's supreme law operates throughout creation. It is involved in the operation of good and evil, in the operation of the psychic and physical realms. He believed Jesus realized that *one law* reigns supreme in the Cosmos and in the life of man. Jesus called its operation the "reign of God." He could not have understood this law as it is understood today, in terms of the second law of thermodynamics. But he could have *realized intuitively* its meaning in terms of the operation of nature, as this truth came to him from his *unconscious* store. Truth cannot be described in the same words from generation to generation because language is constantly created. But truth does speak the same meaning throughout time, because truth's meaning does not change.

In Jesus' day, men had realized that the supreme law involves constant disorganization, and this was expressed as the epitome of man's wisdom in the concept that "this, too, shall pass away." The expected end of the world and of life as man had known it was tantamount then to today's expectation of the heat death of the universe and the end of life within it.

Jesus could have realized then, as a person may today, that the other side of the operation of this same law insures life, although this cannot be readily perceived. Until man understands that life is everlasting, he will not begin to live *in truth*. To learn to live *in truth* is what man must do before a more mature expression of life can come into being. Jesus could have realized then, as a person may today, that evil is the *symbolic word* that denotes the material realm expressed as matter organized to provide the necessary fuel for life.

99

The Stranger says that Jesus gave the answer to the meaning of nature's supreme law (and the source from which he had drawn it) in the Sermon on the Mount when he said, "Seek ye first the kingdom of God [within you], and his righteousness; and all these things shall be added unto you. Take, therefore, no thought for the morrow: for the morrow shall take thought for the things of itself. Sufficient unto the day is the evil thereof."[64] He is saying that knowledge drawn from the kingdom within, the *unconscious*, will provide the knowledge man requires to answer his every need; and the universe operates in time in such manner that there will always be sufficient matter organized as fuel and sufficient psychic energy organized as desire to support life abundantly; and despite the fact that all things pass away, all things are made anew; and "Let there be light" is a command that denotes its constant creation.

When man understands that his own and every other life is everlasting and that each one bears an equal measure of life's evil which must be expended in order that the destructive potential be attenuated, Jesus' words that follow take on new meaning. He says, "Judge not, that ye be not judged. For with what judgment ye judge, ye shall be judged: and with what measure ye mete, it shall be measured to you again."[65]

How shall we judge the evil-doing—the sometimes unconscionable expressions of it—that marks the course of human history? Ignorance leads to evil-doing—ignorance of what the other is suffering, until we have suffered it ourselves. But we must know also that only *insanity* is capable of expressing unconscionable evil; and insanity can take the form of insensate sanity, or what appears to be "cold sanity." We must realize that in the end the expression of evil depletes the evil reserves of the whole species. Why? Empathy brings home the pain of evil-doing to every man who becomes aware of it; he experiences the evil of it himself, and has done with a measure of his own raw lust. Human society cannot arrest the increase of empathy. Ever larger numbers of people are, therefore, experiencing the evil that is being done and are ready to have done with it. Whoever has borne to the grave an unconscionable load of evil, has borne it for humankind, because humanity will not be able to re-express it again, *precisely*.

A person cannot keep his sanity if he commits unconscionable evil. Such a "load of evil" was placed upon Judas that he could not sustain it in sanity. He becomes *symbol* of evil's end result: it is cast into the "potter's field" of consciousness and destroys itself as a force capable of expressing evil again. Jesus did not command Judas to kill himself, but he knew that Judas would not be able to live with himself after the betrayal because of the love between them. Jesus said, "Greater love hath no man than this, that a man lay down his life for his friends. Ye are my friends, if ye do whatsoever I command you."[66] Judas betrayed Jesus, as Jesus had commanded him to do. As Judas betrayed him, Jesus called him *friend*.

No one man can reveal the whole of truth. Jesus understood this, and Judas must have understood that his help was necessary to Jesus to dramatize the story of light in the physical realm, as well as the pattern of the end of sin and evil-doing.

In sharing the responsibility, the privilege, of bringing truth to the consciousness of mankind, Jesus showed that he was the very opposite of a self-deluded Messiah who must be all, reveal all, and thereby corner the power, glory, and grace of life. But he saw his revelation as a necessary step in the development of the consciousness of his own people and the consciousness of the Greco-Roman world in which the seed of Science was trying to flower.

There is no way to explain the persistence of Jesus' message—seemingly so contradictory, and so distorted at the hands of theologians—except to conclude that he evokes devotion in the minds of intelligent men because his drama rings with the sound of truth on every level —material and psychic. Theology cannot destroy the true symbol Jesus made of himself and of every actor who takes a role in the Palestinian mystery play. *True symbols evoke unconscious response and work at subconscious levels to release understanding, regardless of what the superstructures of consciousness and the churches might be saying.*

As we reach today's scene, we cannot tell whether Judaism and Christianity will walk through the door *The Stranger* opens and into a rebirth that will insure the vitality of the Western religions in tomorrow's world. But it is evident that in the developing planetary civilization, Western man cannot present himself as committed to either orthodox Judaic theology or orthodox Christian theology much longer. This is good. Either they will evolve into "temples of understanding" that transcend their exclusiveness and limitations—inviting Islam to follow suit—or these kindred religions will wither. Arnold Toynbee observed that *practice unsupported by belief is a wasting asset.* Western man no longer believes in these theologies.

In Christendom, a growing number of fundamentalists are turning to *new revelations* of Jesus that come through modern mediums or by means of automatic writing.[67] Because such revelations differ in part from the Gospels, and include so much information about the "holy family" as well as people extraneous to the story, they create what may be called a "mystic brand of Form Criticism and Jesus Research." The trouble is, these new revelations differ widely from each other—the question remains of what version of Jesus' story to accept. How do we appraise these new revelations?

Jesus said, "Many shall come in my name, saying, I am Christ; and shall deceive many."[68] But he also said, "For whosoever shall give you a cup of water to drink in my name, because ye belong to Christ, verily I say unto you, he shall not lose his reward."[69] The new revelations are not to be decried—they slake the thirst of those who can neither believe nor relinquish traditional views. But neither can they be accepted as the "Gospel truth."

Granted that it is possible to question the *unconscious* and receive from it true answers, we must still acknowledge that the replies must be given in parable, metaphor, symbolical and allegorical ways—or be rendered too vague for real comprehension—when the questioner is unable to understand the nature of what he has asked or the answer that truth would give. We must also acknowledge that a person's superego transmits the message, clothing it with his own choice of words and coloring it with his consciousness and commitments. Therefore, a person cannot speak in the name of another to the exclusion of himself.

We must conclude that each person who speaks in the name of Jesus is offering simply his own understanding of him, drawn from the heights and depths of his psyche and knowledge.

Harold did not profess to have received any sort of psychic revelation. He speaks neither in his own name, nor in Jesus' name. He speaks in "the name of the Gospels," because he realized that the Gospels must and would remain authoritative insofar as Jesus is concerned. And Harold offers his work only as *his own understanding of the Jesus of the Gospels,* showing how they can be seen to be Jesus' message as he wished to leave it—free of "information" that would becloud the precise symbol he wished to create, and "information" that would serve only to help perpetuate the concepts he strove to transcend and reverse.

Although modern psychic revelations are not without value, they cannot support the sagging Judeo-Christian religions. The Bible cannot be rewritten. This is the record the Western world must contend with. And its popularity, even as a literary masterpiece, is rapidly dwindling.[70]

Harold contends with the *record,* the Bible. Through the pen of this unknown author, the Scriptures and the Jesus of the Gospels have been brought to life in the twentieth century. Following the path that Harold's pen traced, let us now observe Jesus and the Scriptures on the sets where the worldly philosophers and Science hold sway.

ACT THREE

Truth Is the Shining Stranger Mankind Seeks

Science Needs Religion

There is a growing suspicion—and here it is: however far afield traditional Religion may have gone, the general insights into man and nature it provides are in closer touch with reality than those Science is offering.

Because Preston Harold's devotion to Science equaled his devotion to Religion, he strove to unite these two forces—not for the sake of Religion so much as for the sake of Science and mankind. He saw that today the world is desperately in need of a reinterpretation of natural laws and phenomena. Irrational and nihilistic scientific doctrines are misleading man; scientists are unintentionally devastating man's faith in himself and in the universe. Because scientists tend to demean life, their promises are arid. But *Science remains the last best hope* in man's search for truth. Dr. Robert M. L. Baker, Jr., defines Science as: "The systematization of knowledge and quest for truth, including ever more general laws, as motivated by curiosity."

Science is the quest for truth, and its influence staggers the imagination. This is why a more penetrating and comprehensive view of the findings of Science—a view that generates a new philosophy of Science, a new cosmology, a new view of man—is the crying need of the world.

But first, let us take a look at the irrationality of the scientific view of man and the universe that holds sway today—the view that is undermining meaning and purpose in life.

Science poses itself as man's best hope and salvation. But hope and salvation become meaningless *in principle,* the possibility that there is salvation or reason for hope is repudiated, when many scientists state that the universe is dying.

Science preaches and attempts to practice the highest ethic, demanding to share its knowledge freely. It commands the whole of society to do likewise. Then it announces that behavior is so conditioned that there is little if any choice in the matter of a person's belief and behavior.

Scientists demand that war cease in the name of human morality and the preciousness of human life. Yet, scientists proclaim that man is no more than the product of a blind and purposeless nature in which such moral attitudes can neither exist nor be commanded. In nature, creatures must kill and be killed; might is right, whether it be the might of the parasite or the lion; the crippled or helpless must be abandoned, devil take the hindmost.

If man and a cabbage are siblings of insensate energy, scientists might as well call upon vegetation to stop rotting as to call upon man to stop polluting his environment. Either man is a superior and special product of Cosmic mind and energy, or it is ridiculous to demand more of mankind than animalistic behavior.

In short, nihilistic Science renders itself and all attempts at social progress inane. If in principle there is no purpose, no meaning, no rewarding goal toward which evolution progresses in individual and in universal terms, then Science has no meaning, and it matters not whether man's flame of consciousness, caught in an insensate universe, is snuffed out.

The nihilistic view is irrational, because it does not conform to the data Science has amassed. The facts keep pointing to the conclusion that although man inhabits a natural body, he is altogether different from every other expression in nature—and the formulation of Science and technology is itself the best proof of this view. The facts also keep pointing to the conclusion that scientists scarcely know more about the universe than a fetus knows about the world; life in the womb may be coming to an end, but it is coming to a beginning in a wider sphere of being. The facts also keep pointing to the conclusion that the real nature of energy is not yet understood; it is too early in the day of knowledge to rule out the probability that there is a converse process that balances the disorganization of energy.

Science is irrational because the great majority of scientists feel within themselves that the marvel of the Cosmos is not the product of blind forces moving toward senseless, lifeless motion—and neither is man. The deeper they delve, the greater their reverence for the order they behold, the greater the mystery of "energy," the more similarity they find between the underlying patterns of organic and inorganic expressions of energy, and the more evident it becomes that man must and will express God-consciousness, even though he refuses outgrown theologies. Scientists who should be leading the world into a new religious concept of

Cosmic dimension too often pay lip service to nihilistic doctrines they do not really believe but are too cautious to repudiate. These doctrines create the "mental smog" that hangs heavy, heavy over the head of man, although he may not be aware of the source of it.

Scientists, like theologians, have become so doctrinaire, so exclusive, that those who seek to know the truth of inner space and psychic energy as well as the truth of outer space and physical energy, must seek elsewhere. For the most part, parapsychology and metaphysics are shunned.

The whole picture is confounded. There is a loss of understanding of causality in the various disciplines. The world that Science studies is bound up by cause-and-effect relationships with the world in which Religion has meaning because, as Einstein realized, the observer is a part of the observation. This takes us back to an early battle between Science and Religion—the question of whether the earth revolves around the sun or vice versa. The real question was not so much whether the earth is the center of the universe as whether Cosmic (God's) attention is centered upon man. Religion insisted that man is central to the issue, whatever the issue may be. Now Science admits that this is true. As we understand the structure of the universe today, the center of it has no real meaning; but recognizing the role of the observer in making observations does have meaning. Genesis says that the observer's role, Adam's role, is the central role in the process of observation and "naming" or *understanding* the forces of nature over which he is to gain dominion. Therefore, each man is *a* center of Cosmic concern. *The Stranger* says, "If man is the most highly developed form of life, the only speaking creature in the universe, then in the most profound sense of the word, the earth is the 'center' of it."[71] Certainly, earth is *a* "brain child" of the Cosmos, such as Reiser envisions our planet to be.

It is time for Science to take a deeper look into religious expression.

Is there an ancient and *intuitive* understanding of DNA–RNA, which takes the shape of a coil, a double helix, a spiral, and is today known to be the "very stuff" of life? Genesis says that the "play of energy" that leads to the expression of life is "serpent"—a coiling action—involving an "intertwining" code script (the tree of knowledge of good and evil and the tree of life), so that *a double helix and spiraling form is basic in energy's expression.*

If scientists will look again at the legend of Adam, Eve, Cain, and Abel, they will see that it describes in a *poetic way* the operation of nature's supreme law with astonishing accuracy. It tells us that as the energy source (Adam-Eve) goes to *work*, heat is a "by-product" of what is produced (Cain slays Abel in the heat of anger). In this operation, a measure of energy (Abel) is lost, "buried" in the "field" of matter. And the organization of the energy involved changes in a way that increases the "random element" (Cain wandering in the wilderness). The legend tells us that in time, source energy (Adam-Eve) is reorganized in such way that replacement energy is introduced into the system to allow it to continue its operation (Seth comes as "replacement seed" and through him manifest energy continues to be organized, disorganized, and reorganized). The legend indicates that there is a centering of energy or power in *one* "atom of action" (Seth). This one "quantum of energy" produced by parent source plays the commanding role in its house. But we may also see that the "random element" (Cain) plays a constructive role in producing the ongoing manifestations of energy because his force is reorganized. The "wave trains" (progeny) emanating from this opposing frequency (Cain) cross-act (intermarry or "constructively interfere") with the "wave trains" (progeny) emanating from the *one* that is playing the commanding role (Seth) to provide the ongoing propagation of Israel, the "wave group" that brings "light" (Jesus) into expression.

Harold believed that the laws and findings of the sciences are simply *developments in the expression of truth* that has been intuitively grasped and poetically stated in the great religions. He believed that as Jesus studied the Scriptures he saw in them the same thing he, Harold, saw in them and also in the records of Jesus' drama: these writings embody a symbolical representation of the underlying laws functioning throughout nature.

Harold saw that with each enlargement of the boundaries of consciousness, man's ability to *describe* his realizations of the reality that underlies appearances and the principles that operate throughout nature has become more precise because of the development of more exact language and better mathematics. But reality itself does not change. Progress in describing reality equals progress in mathematics, which gives a precise and unambiguous description such as words and early symbols could not convey.

Harold was the first to measure Jesus' description of the realm of God and its working (and what is this realm and reign, if not the Cosmos and energy operating within it?) against the description of nature's supreme law and the basic laws of physics. He showed that, in every particular, Jesus' poetic words and the symbols he used are harmonious, congruent in every way, with the scientists' understanding of the "reign" of the second law of thermodynamics in the physical realm; and with the principle of indeterminacy, and the principle of detailed balancing; and with the concept of field energy, with the Lorentz-Fitzgerald contraction, with light quanta and other paradoxical mysteries of physics too numerous to name.[72] Here are three examples:

(1) About two thousand years after Jesus, scientists discovered that nature's supreme law gives rise to a *measurable property*, and to the concept of *chance* versus *adverse chance* (or probability that the law might fail). The measurable property is involved with the action of energy throughout the universe, and is so vast in its reach and implications that man cannot yet comprehend its actual meaning. *Adverse chance*, on the other hand, is *so small* that if it were written out in decimal notation the number of significant figures would be *so large* that (as Eddington puts it) all the books in the world could not hold it. Jesus described Cosmic operation in terms of the kingdom and reign of God. He likened the operation of the "system" to a seed, which involves the action of energy, and said that "this measure" or seed is *smaller than any on earth* and grows to be *larger than any plant*. Therefore, the "measure" of the fundamental aspects of the "reign of God" (or nature's supreme law operating throughout the universe, the kingdom of God) is not readily conceivable in ordinary "earthly" terms.

(2) Think of all the discussion today about the curvature of space. In the play of physical energy there are no absolutely straight lines; think of all we know about the many *interpenetrating fields of energy* in which *particlelike motions* occur; think of the energy flowing through space. Is there a better description of this Cosmic structure and play of energy than to say, as Jesus did of the kingdom and reign of God, that it is like a *net cast into the sea* that holds *fish* ("particlelike motions") of all sorts? Today we know the limitations of Euclidean geometry, which in Jesus' day described reality in terms that might be likened to a net stretched taut, upon which perfect spheres were balanced. But, Jesus himself, whether in childhood or in manhood, must have had a vision of energy's "dancing" lines, flowing apart, coming together, bisecting, in a flow or curving motion, as do the lines of a net in the sea.

(3) What is the actual wealth that a particle of energy represents really like? Jesus said that it is like treasure buried in a field. Scientists cannot give you a better answer today, but they would point out something that Jesus also pointed out in parable so long ago. *You cannot at the same time "possess" both the particle and its place of being.* To do so, you would have to determine both its position and its velocity, and

these measurements cannot be obtained with complete certainty simultaneously. In Jesus' explanation, once you know that the "treasure" is buried in the field, you must be off to purchase the field. Therefore, you do not simultaneously and with certainty possess both the treasure and its place of being. The position and velocity of the treasure and of yourself are involved. The treasure is always elusive. You find the perfect "pearl of high price," but you must then be off to "sell all you have" to purchase it. Again, you do not simultaneously and with certainty possess both the treasure and its place of being. The treasure is never exactly pinpointed.

Jesus presented himself as *symbol of light, insisting that he must be understood in terms of one, only*. All that man knows about light and its actions tells him that there is a centering of energy, light, or power in *one measure* (the quantum), and a transferring of energy from the unapparent underlying source of it into light wave groups, or quanta, which somehow are enfolded by and then are subject to release by atomic matter with which they interact. Jesus' words and drama symbolize the whole complicated and paradoxical story of the quantum and light wave group so correctly that it is astounding. Consider now that if he were accurately to symbolize light and its propagation, his "story" as given in the Gospels must be as seemingly contradictory, paradoxical, and strange as is the "story" of light's functioning in the physical world. If the Gospels were not contradictory, paradoxical—strangely so—they would not conform to the "story" of light, in the inner and outer worlds, which is what Jesus' revelation is all about. To Harold, this was why Jesus, through use of posthypnotic response and recall, saw to it that his record was given as he wished it given regardless of the controversy such conflicting reports must engender.

That Jesus' story and utterances could have so perfectly threaded the course of modern physics by "accident" would call for "fortuitous chance" beyond anyone's ability to calculate. It is to be expected that scientists are reluctant to relate Jesus' message to nature's underlying operations and laws. But strange, is it not, that orthodox Christians who believe that Jesus was the only incarnation of God to come upon the earth appear unable to believe that *God in the flesh* could have an understanding of the all-pervading operation of the second law of thermodynamics. Or that He (as God) might devote Himself to describing the working of this law in the only way it might come in time to be understood—in poetic, symbolic words which, Jesus said, described the reign of *the* law that could not fail and the working of energy within God's kingdom, the Cosmos. Would not God in the flesh of one man understand also the secret of light's propagation?

Whatever orthodox theologians may think of Harold's interpretation of Jesus and his mission, it is to be hoped that they will recognize the value of the parallels drawn between Jesus' strange words and the laws of modern physics in Chapters Six through Nine of *The Shining Stranger*. It is also to be hoped that they will use these parallels to show that, however one regards the Nazarene, *he was in touch with reality in all its depths, that what he said is more relevant and meaningful in today's world than it could possibly have been to his own generation.*

What is the answer to the mystery of Jesus' poetic description of these complex laws and the phenomena that confront physicists? Reason would have us conclude that the underlying patterns in nature are similar and that there are *parallels of operation in the physical and psychical realms.* Therefore, anyone who could draw upon his *unconscious* to reveal the dynamics of man's inward kingdom would in the same "telling" reveal the dynamics of Cosmic operation. *The Stranger* says:

> It is not essential to concede that Jesus understood physical phenomena and mathematics as such—it is necessary only to concede that truth pre-exists and inescapably imposes the path to be followed, and that the *unconscious* in man has direct access to truth, and that Jesus knew how to tap this fount within himself, letting it express through him and direct his drama.[73]

Jesus was not the only man to draw upon the fount of truth that flows in the depths of man and to then utilize the symbols that arise as guiding images to lead him to a deeper understanding of nature's operations.

Many scientists have acknowledged the "kingdom within" to be the source from which their discoveries were drawn. Here, briefly, is the story of a great scientist who also saw energy "dancing" with his inner eye. Dr. Ira Progoff tells about August Kekulé in *Depth Psychology and Modern Man*. Kekulé's discoveries were of greatest importance for the development of both applied and theoretical organic chemistry. In 1890 he gave a speech in which Progoff says he described "some of the intimate experiences that led him to his discoveries; and these are of very great significance for our understanding of the depth processes that operate in the psyche of the creative scientist." Kekulé said:

> It is said that a genius recognizes truth without knowing the evidence for it. I do not doubt that even in ancient times this kind of thinking occurred. Would Pythagoras have offered up a hecatomb if he had recognized his famous theorem only after finding a way to prove it?

Progoff comments, "New insights do not depend on the outward observations, measurements, and analyses of the subject matter. The crucial step in gaining the new knowledge comes from within, and its validity may be perceived, or at least *felt*, before it can be outwardly proved." Kekulé said that while on a bus ride across London:

> I fell into a reverie, and lo, the atoms were gamboling before my eyes! Whenever, hitherto, these diminutive beings had appeared to me, they had always been in motion; but up to that time I had never been able to discern the nature of their motion. Now, however, I saw how, frequently, two smaller atoms united to form a pair; how a larger one embraced the two smaller ones; how still larger ones kept hold of three or even four of the smaller; whilst the whole kept whirling in a giddy dance. . . . This was the origin of the "Structural Theory."

Progoff says, "He tells us that in times past he had permitted himself to fall into a reverie in order to 'see' the inner workings of the atom before his mind's eye," and he realized that he "must move deeper into the subliminal levels of his psyche than he had done in previous reveries," if he were to see these workings in the detail that his scientific knowledge required. It was after this that his second great discovery, the benzene-ring theory, was made. He was dozing before the fire:

> Again the atoms were gamboling before my eyes. . . . My mental eye, rendered more acute by repeated visions of this kind, could now distinguish larger structures of manifold conformation; long rows, sometimes more closely fitted together all twining and twisting in snake-like motion. But look! What was that? One of the snakes had seized hold of its own tail and the form whirled mockingly before my eyes. As if by a flash of lightning I awoke; and this time also I spent the rest of the night in working out the consequences of the hypothesis. . . . Let us learn to dream, gentlemen, then perhaps we shall learn the truth.[74]

Here, we see that the ancient religious symbol of the serpent appeared again in the mind of a perceptive man who then precised its meaning in the modern language of chemistry and mathematics.

Before Kekulé's time, before Jesus' time, many drew forth truth from the kingdom within and expressed it in the language and symbols of the day with such perfect and poetic precision that the sacred books of all religions become a mother lode upon which Science can draw. And Science is in desperate need of something to draw upon.

Science now confronts an impasse as formidable as theology's, because it has come face to face with that which is as inexplicable as the Holy Ghost—the real nature of energy. Splitting energy into elementary particles to penetrate deeper into the make-up of the "stuff" leads to an impasse, because there is nothing small enough to penetrate the least active of the elementary particles, the neutrinos. There are two types of neutrinos, which are identical except that they have opposite spin. The one is not the antiparticle of the other, for each has its own antiparticle. Both are stable. They are produced in the decay of larger particles, but they themselves do not decay. A Science committed to the theory of the "heat death" of the universe sees them as the "ashes" of energy. They permeate our environment just about as consistently as does space itself.

To Preston Harold, they were the veritable "stuff" of the universe—the Adam and Eve of energy, the alpha and omega of it, which means that through these particles all is created anew. He saw them as nature's building blocks or "tiniest pair of hands." They provide the basis for a new definition of God, which is implicit in Harold's writings, but it was put into words by Frederic Lassiter:

> God is an irreducible number of indestructible elementary particles, being everywhere present, out of which everything is made.

In order for this definition to conform completely to Harold's concepts, it would be necessary to substitute *neutrinos* for *elementary particles*. *Everything made* must include the creation of space, derived from a particular expression of this energy, and it would be necessary to add that God is all that these indestructible particles are *not*, which means energy too finely drawn to be considered in terms of a material particle, however minute, to which we give the name of mental energy, but derived from the same source of Cosmic energy from which the particles were drawn. This mental energy was called the Word in Jesus' revelation. It is called the Cosmic Imagination by Oliver Reiser.

Science keeps coming face to face with Jesus' poetic words. If what a person says keeps coming true, there is good reason to believe that he knows what he is talking about.

We are on the verge of catching up with Jesus' view of evolution. Evolution is involved in his doctrine because he presented mankind as child. This must mean that man is growing, changing, evolving into what he is going to become. Jesus also insisted that mankind is *more* than the rest of nature's expressions, and that this has been true since the beginning. Therefore, Harold presented man as a *parallel* development in nature, to a degree self-conscious and, therefore, God-conscious from amoebic state onward, guided by an inner force or light that took man into and out of nature's stymied forms and led him to the pinnacle of its development. Now, hear this:

In March of 1969, Dr. Louis S. B. Leakey discussed his finds that once again scramble the pieces of the puzzle of man's evolution: "Recently unearthed fossil bones indicate that both a very early man and a very early gorilla coexisted in Africa 20 million years ago. . . . Even then, both man and gorilla were advancing along different and separate evolutionary paths. . . . Man descended along with the apes, not from them." Dr. Leakey also observed that we must either change the definition of man as "toolmaker" or invite the chimpanzees to send a representative to the United Nations, because "toolmaker" is no longer a valid definition for man—chimpanzees fashion primitive tools, and teach their young to use them.[75]

Noting that chimpanzees, man's closest "relatives," do not *speak* and cannot be taught even to try to speak (although they communicate primitive messages "intelligently" via sound waves), Harold had long since changed the definition of man. *The Stranger* says, "All in creation is alive, and may be seen as the 'flesh' of the living God to be used with intelligence and compassion. But the mind that thinks to speak is abstracted from all living material except man. Man did not inherit the power of the word from the animal kingdom; speech was initiated in him. . . . Is possession of this power synonymous with possession of life itself, *in reality*, as opposed to being living material to some degree conscious as is a proton or a gorilla? The opening verses of the Gospel of St. John define life and God in terms of the *word*: the word was God, in the word 'was life; and the life was the light of men.' By this definition, *life* can be ascribed only to man."[76] Life can be defined only in terms of man, and man can be defined only in terms of the power of the word—speech, reading, writing. It is very probable that scientists will create living material in their test tubes; but it is very improbable that they will ever create *life*. All that there is of *life* was created in the beginning, and is evolving in a parallel process with universal evolution.

A Science that seeks to understand the secret of life as opposed to the mechanisms by which living material comes into being and operates must seek first the "kingdom" within man, because herein it finds the only contact there is with the reality that *was* in the beginning of the evolutionary process and the reality that *now* underlies appearances.

Mental and mathematical concepts, such as the neutrinos are, have brought Science to a new level of understanding. Now, a "quantum jump" is called for. Science will be able to make it when scientists realize that *man is the book* in which the secrets of the Cosmos are written. This means that the anthropomorphic view must be taken, and completely taken. In the past, the anthropomorphic approach has singled out the male in his prime as conveyor of nature's whole pattern. What about the "little ones" and the very ancient? What is the meaning of woman enfolded in man's being? Does not this make mankind an expression that is *parallel to the neutrinos*—divided into like but opposite particles that are equal in every way except in the direction of "spin"? How much of this neutral energy, and in what arrangement, does it take to express a male or positive charge, or a female or negative charge?—the proton, or electron?

Many scientists have seen that Science will come to terms with the anthropomorphic view. Teilhard de Chardin was one of them. Such a view leads to the "Divine Materialism" that Harold ascribed to Jesus.[77] Only by taking a completely anthropomorphic view can we see the earth as a planetary body with a World Sensorium that communicates with itself and with the Cosmos as it responds to and resonates with the divine Cosmic Imagination. The earth becomes as one person (Adam-Eve), the Cosmos becomes as God, in the same one-to-one correspondence as Genesis portrays between God and man and as Jesus said existed between each human being and God.

True scientists grow humble, meek of heart, when they confront their own ignorance as opposed to the majesty and mystery of the Cosmos. Who, then, shall inherit the earth? Coming generations who will be guided by the methodology and ethics of Science, when it has opened itself to the study of God-consciousness in man and man's psychic powers.

Otto Rank saw that the will to immortality is the strongest force operating in humankind.[78] Jesus' doctrine is the doctrine of everlasting life. Did he see as Rank did that *immortality is mankind's goal* and that *because of this* man's evolving consciousness will achieve it? But first, man must determine what kind of society he really wants and what it is that brings real satisfaction in life.

Human Nature Dictates the Course
Economy and Government Follow

For several centuries past, the crusade toward human dignity and freedom has been led by those who spend their lives on the political scene,
wrangling with the problems of the day. Harold calls them "political
saints" and says that there are more than can be counted in each country,
in each period of history. Because of them, the world stands on the
brink of hope.

Many will shudder, many will applaud when they read the name of
Karl Marx in the category of political saints, which includes such men
as Thomas Jefferson and Abraham Lincoln. But the capitalism that Marx
experienced and repudiated along with all its trappings was a disgrace
to humanity—it was doomed to change or die, once the force of Marx's
pen had been turned against it. It changed and is still changing. It would
be difficult to determine how much humanity owes this man, despite
the evil that has been done in his name. Capitalistic countries are most
in his debt. He forced them into a more ethical practice—made capitalism a more ethical system, if ethical is to be measured in terms of
actual ownership by the greatest number of people of the means of pro-
duction and the goods produced.

Much poverty remains in capitalistic countries, but people also have
much control over their lives. This does not mean that the poor should
count their blessings; it means that the system in which they live has
not yet completely corrected itself, but that it is capable of doing so and
at a rapid pace. Communism, too, changes. But not so rapidly. The cross-
fertilization continues and works to the advantage of all.

But what both the capitalistic and the communistic worlds are coming
to see is that the trouble in this planetary society is not traceable to
economic malpractices so much as it is traceable to what may be called

malpractice of religious concepts—especially the religious ideal of the brotherhood of man. This ideal receives little more than lip service in both worlds.

The validity of the brotherhood of man must rest upon the principle of the Fatherhood of God and the unique endowment of each person, which elevates him to a very special place in nature and puts each human being into one-to-one correspondence with each other human being. This principle makes each person worthy of every consideration that would be shown to one who is considered to be the summit of human greatness. Unless man is born of One Parent Energy (God), and unless he is uniquely endowed, "brotherhood" extends throughout nature, giving society the right and reason to treat the brothers as they treat any beast of burden, barnyard fowl, or insect.

Neither atheism nor a pantheism that denies the uniqueness of man can support the ideal of the brotherhood of man, which commands for the lowliest equal dignity, opportunity, and the other rights and blessings humanity aspires to. A society that disavows Religion, God, limits itself to the law and society of the jungle in which *fear keeps constant company with beauty*. Or the society may pattern itself after the barnyard or the antheap. But it has built into it limiting ideas that prohibit its evolution into a society that is better than any nature has produced, including those societies that man has brought forth thus far.

The cardinal error of Marx was to repudiate God. He should rather have repudiated the oppressive and irrational theology of his day, thus leaving the door open for an evolution of man's understanding of God-consciousness in himself, which is as much a part of him as self-consciousness is and commands him to exercise *freedom and responsibility*. In time, the communistic world will correct this error.

In the capitalistic world, failure to practice the doctrine of Jesus, which insists upon the preciousness of each human life, the equal potential of every person, is at the root of our troubles. In truth, we have failed to educate "even the least of these, my brethren"—in spirit, we have failed to appreciate the richness of their contribution to the cultural life of the nation, failed to accord them justice, opportunity, dignity, and brotherly love. Paternalism is intolerable. The religions of the West have been saying this (although failing to comprehend the message) for as long as they have told the story of the paternalistic state of mankind in Eden, which God (Cosmic mind) *set the stage to destroy* in order that mankind might come into his own and live—and from which God drove mankind when they rose to the "bait" and acted in accordance with human nature. The legend says that man will not acquit himself in a responsible way when he is locked in paternalistic bondage. Freedom evokes responsibility.

The discrimination that is at the root of all discrimination is inequality between the sexes and discrimination against the female, which reduces her to the status of chattel. The first equality was, and must again be, mankind equal to *itself*. Eve was not a female person. Vinciata (Joseph Wallace King) has painted a true portrait of Adam's "rib"—a feminine being with no navel. Eve, actually, is the feminine aspect of the consciousness of each person. Neither Eve nor Adam considered separately represents Homo sapiens in the legend.

As men degrade the women of their race, they are degrading the *race* and themselves—socially, mentally, emotionally—because they are degrading the feminine aspect of their psyche. The same is true as regards women degrading their men. But more often in human history the reverse has been true—and continues to be true. Woman has been treated as a *thing* in too many societies, and she has, therefore, too often allowed herself to be used as such. As a person possesses a thing, it possesses him, and so the sexes have tended to entrap each other.[79]

The Stranger says that the Genesis legend reveals the primordial misuse of the human being that is at the root of all misuse of people. It is misuse of man by his *brother-being*: Cain's murder of Abel, and man's enslavement of mankind that threads through the ensuing story.[80] This points to the fact that a people must first misuse *its own kind* before other peoples can misuse them. Each sex must first misuse itself before the opposite sex can misuse it.

Harold says that mankind must first become equal to itself, woman equal to man, before there can be equality among all peoples.

Today, mankind faces the necessity of coming to grips with the truth presented by Jesus and echoed in the words of Walt Whitman, "Whoever degrades another degrades me, and whatever is done or said returns at last to me."[81] The society of the future will shape itself upon this precept, because this is the truth of human nature, and human nature itself will dictate the course society must follow. Social organization is the "tool" that mankind is now shaping. It is a tool that must be fashioned to serve him as he serves life well, and also serves himself.

Law is actually the most powerful and constructive implement that man has fashioned. *Government under law was the promised land toward which Moses led Israel.* But, like any tool, law must be cleansed of time's accretions; it must be made workable. If it is to meet with the need and

117

nature of man, it must evolve apace with the evolution of his consciousness. And so must the economic system man operates. Jesus recognized both necessities.

Jesus concerned himself with life in this world. His parables present a pattern of economic practice which shows that the course man's nature leads him to follow traces the same path, whatever the name he gives the operation or the political superstructure. Economic history has followed the pattern these parables present, as Harold shows in Chapter Seventeen of *The Shining Stranger*. Jesus did not name his economic doctrine, but the principles he stated must be identified with those associated with capitalism. Jesus' economic principles are both ethical and dynamic, geared to producing abundance—not merely to meeting need.

Technology promises abundance, whether the technology is developed by capitalistic or communistic societies. But Harold saw that men deceive themselves when they believe that affluence or economic development by itself has or will determine the history-making process by which any "ism" will be settled. Human nature demands *more*. This is what Jesus understood. He saw that although man seeks always to profit himself, the psychological rewards and costs outweigh the material rewards and costs. Jesus synthesized his economic doctrine: "For what shall it profit a man, if he shall gain the whole world, and lose his own soul?"[82]

Affluence in itself does not rob a man of his soul, but any system that makes him first of all a creature of the State, its chattel, does rob him of it. Harold believed that Jesus espoused the profit system upon which capitalism depends because he saw that "*each person is his own first capital-good. He must realize a profit upon this capital: himself, his life,* rather than working for his keep as does slave or animal. One lends himself to his job, may invest himself as heavily as he will in his work, must insist upon a premium for his efforts, and this in addition to the return of his capital: himself as a free agent. His demanding a return on money, capital investment, allows him to insist upon a wage or interest that will constitute a profit on his labor. His money represents his or another's labor—as he invests it, he must demand both interest and the return of his capital if he is to demand a premium for his efforts and freedom for himself. . . . In simple truth, *man cannot escape capitalism for he, himself, is capital-good*,"[83] and therefore to take a dispirited view of private enterprise and the capitalistic system is to take a dispirited view of man.

The Stranger says that opportunity, as opposed to enslavement or coercion, creation in addition to mere labor, and *a society structured to meet the needs of those who for any reason cannot or will not respond to opportunity* will meet the nature and need of man. There will always be those who cannot or will not compete, but for the vast majority, a chance to work and to create will elicit their efforts. Harold saw that "opportunity involves a chance to compete, and a certain degree of competition appears to be a necessary ingredient to insure real achievement, as well as to give the bread by which man lives a satisfactory taste."[84] Now listen to this:

> A study of suicides in both literate and non-literate societies shows that societies with a high suicide rate appear to be characterized by a placid, cooperative and uncompetitive style of life.
>
> Professor Stuart Palmer, a University of New Hampshire sociologist, conducted the study. He also observes that these societies do not stress individualism, but are community-oriented instead. He finds that those societies with a low suicide rate stress moderate competition and individualism. . . .[85]

Acquiring a "Group-ego" will never satisfy man's need to seek and follow his own Authority-Ego, the Divine Absence of himself. Eden-like provision for man's every need only drives him to desperation, saps his will to live and meet the challenges of life. But in today's world, these challenges must be tempered, or otherwise they would be overwhelming.

We do not have to resort to *either* capitalism *or* communism. There are wider possibilities. Society may take the shape of organization that provides for the needs of the human race, every member to be held precious, and also provides for the opportunity to compete, create, and turn a profit on one's life whether the profit be measured in psychological or material gain.

Marx did not believe a real and honest profit was to be made. He saw profit only as money squeezed from the laborer who can produce in a day more than it takes to provide his keep—and in Marx's day, the laborer was paid no more than enough to keep him. Marx also believed that the "correct" price of a product was its calculable labor value. Harold took another view of pricing and profit. *The Stranger* says:

> . . . from the day Homo sapiens began his operation of the market, each thing he could produce and sell could rightly be sold for more than the amount of calculable labor the article represents; and real profit is to be realized as accrued labor-value gives rise to improved tools and methods which allow for more to be produced in less time and with less work. . . . an incalculable amount goes to the consumer as gift from the past, even as a calculable amount is charged as profit.[86]

Matter is not "dead stuff"—even an elementary particle is "conscious" of its like and opposite kind of charge. And the things that man makes of this "living material" incorporate something of the life of the one who shapes them.

Jesus appreciated the living quality of things, and he realized that things possess a person in the spirit in which he possesses them. *The Stranger* says, "One might say that Jesus was 'housed' in His robe— and that the difference between the tortoise who wears his home and a person in his home is only one of degree. A man's home reflects his being, his possessions reveal him, and if there is nothing he can in truth call his own he cannot in truth call his soul his own, for his soul must have a *housing*. . . . Jesus' doctrine comes to rest in the concept that man cannot view mammon supinely nor use mammon dishonestly and reap a profit on his life. He damns the damnable with candor, and commands man to pluck out, to cast off, the offensive in himself. He teaches that when a man is honest and friendly in his dealings with and usage of mammon, things, the material realm, mammon serves him well. . . ."[87] Man cannot serve mammon, because mammon is here to serve man. Jesus saw that as man uses mammon, he serves life, and as man serves life, he serves *God*.

Listen now to *The Stranger*: "Human frailty and human nature bring to bear upon the practice of any system. But as Frederic Bastiat saw in 1848, the danger is that men will pay too much attention to the imperfections of the profit system and will sacrifice their freedom to dictatorial authoritarianism, or what he saw to be the evil of socialism, in its stead. In the words of Heilbroner:

> He began a book entitled *Economic Harmonies* in which he was to show that the apparent disorder of the world was a disorder of the surface only; that underneath, the impetus of a thousand different self-seeking agents became transmuted in the market place into a higher social good. . . .

Jesus calls mammon 'unrighteous' but He, too, appears to have seen that self-serving becomes transmuted in the market place for He says, 'Make to yourselves friends of the mammon of unrighteousness. . . .' This is to say, know the working of nature's physical realm and of the mundane economic world. The temporal, which is mammon, *serves life.* . . . That which is unrighteous in life's operation, mammon, gives way in time to the righteous, to the truth in being which calls man to self-service in the most enlightened sense of the word, that his life may be of profit to himself *in reality, which means that it must also be of profit to his fellowman.*"[88]

Harold believed that the market system, operating at some level in terms of private enterprise, will persist in the society mankind evolves because people enjoy buying and selling and turning a profit. And in the new market that leisure will open, enjoyment will tend to be reinitiated into work. But there is another and more important reason that led Harold to this belief. This is the place of the market system, the profit system, in the evolution of life and society from amoeba to Homo sapiens. *The Stranger* says:

> Man brought forth this system himself. It is unprecedented in the animal world and therefore in line with the whole development of the cell of life that became Homo sapiens. It is the newest economic system under the sun, and as with any powerful new idea or tool, it must be tempered and disciplined before the real profit in it is to be fully realized. Underlying the profit system, upon which capitalism depends, is a principle which in the view of this study led Jesus to espouse it: He saw that the capitalistic system cannot in truth profit itself by malpractice, and thus it tends toward the ethical in its best self-interest and must come in the end to measure its worth in moral and aesthetic as well as material terms.[89]

This is the lesson the capitalistic world is learning today.

In commanding man to render unto Caesar that which is Caesar's, Jesus commanded mankind to recognize the need for government and to support it. In these poetic words, he also indicates that a people who will not support a government that operates apart from Religion will not render unto God his due—which is cooperation with their fellowman. *The Stranger* says:

> Government is communal business that must accrue a profit and invest capital to expand its services to include all of its people and improve their lot. . . . In any type society the world has ever known, however, there is a degree of uncertainty as to whether the needs of the populace will be met. . . . As men deal with the uncertainty problem, the mathematical theory of communication could teach a valuable lesson; the uncertainty that arises from *freedom of choice* is desirable uncertainty— which is to say, to put security, stability, certainty above all else is to trade precious freedom for a myth because actual security does not exist and cannot be guaranteed.[90]

Pause to consider again the message from Eden.

The Eden legend tells us that neither affluence nor security—not even the *assurance of survival*—could satisfy the questing consciousness of

121

man. His primordial instinct, the most compelling one, is to know the secrets of life. He must know enough to provide him with what might be called the first freedom—the freedom of choice. He must exercise this freedom, even if he brings evil upon himself in doing so, because freedom is the most precious of life's attributes.

But freedom of choice is a limited freedom, because human beings cannot realize their potentialities except through the means that organized society provides. The paramountcy of the individual is limited by the need of maintaining and improving social organization. Organization is a tool, nothing more. And civilization progresses as the tools man devises are improved. Jesus understood that truth would prevail, and in the long run only the Religion and only the social organization that meets with the truth of man's nature and need will prevail, because it will command humanity's wholehearted support without coercion.

This optimum society will evolve as empathy evolves, commanding a response that is both unconsciously tempered and in accord with the reality of the situation. Only through empathy is it possible to step into another's shoes without displacing him, or foisting oneself upon him, or losing one's own precious identity. Empathy not only makes this possible, it makes it mandatory. In empathy—loving oneself and loving one's neighbor as he loves himself—rests the hope of the world, in which all are now neighbors. Jesus' great command shows that man can love his neighbor only to the degree that he loves himself, and *as* he loves himself. This poses as the first necessity, in establishing a desirable society, the restoration of self-love and self-respect in each sex and in all of the races of man.

The curtain is more than halfway drawn over the twentieth-century scene as it holds the stage in *The Palestinian Mystery Play*. Power no longer rides supreme. Arms are self-defeating, contradictory in their might. The great powers are as Goliaths posed against many Davids who have for weapon but a pebble. *The Stranger* says:

> Man's helplessness at the height of his power presents the concept that truth when fully stated must conclude in contradictory truths of equal magnitude—in a bifurcation, a forking outward from the penultimate point of truth so that the end of it cannot be reached save as point that opens itself to question, requiring judgment in order to settle the issue or to act upon either the one or the other premise it projects. Thus, no one *final* or *absolute* statement of objective truth can be made. Law may be seen as a penultimate point of objective truth that opens itself to question requiring that judgment be exercised. Today's truth or contradiction in magnitude, seen as man's power versus man's helpless-

ness, comes to rest upon the question of whether he will accept law as the means of governing and settling disputes. . . . When ancestral creature picked up a stick to use for weapon and bequeathed to man his sword, he did his being-duty: only by fashioning a weapon could he survive, rise above the animal kingdom, and be different from it by refusing to evolve into, or in himself *be*, a physical weapon as all other creatures are to greater or lesser degree. Because their swords are built into them their threat to each other persists generation after generation so that fear and enmity are reborn in each species and between neighboring species. Man alone can lay down or pick up his sword. Man can be friend or foe, can love his neighbor as himself. . . .

This civilization may be destroyed in one last conflagration. But twentieth-century man may not destroy his civilization. Enough men may come to see that no "tree" can produce its fruit before, in the natural course of events, the tree is ready to bear it; they may come to see that "rear guard" action allows for retreat instead of chaotic rout as humanity withdraws from its old positions; they may see that opposition is as necessary to effect real progress as antithesis is to effect synthesis. Enough men may come to see that man's consciousness is fluid, and thus he cannot, will not, move against the natural law that water seeks its own level. Empathy, and lack of empathy, divides men into classes, endeavors, and attitudes that support their need to avoid or to join in, to know or not to know, to oppose or to assist. But empathy itself is a gathering force. It will not forever divide. . . .[91]

Willis W. Harman observes that there is mounting evidence to say that we have undersold man, underestimated his possibilities, and misunderstood what is needed for him to make the transition that these times demand. The evidence indicates that—let Harman say it:

> . . . the most profound revolution of the educational system would not be the cybernation of knowledge transmission, but the infusion of an exalted image of what man can be and the cultivation of an enhanced self-image in each individual child. . . . The solution to the alienation and widespread disaffection in our society is not alone in vast social programs, but will come about through widespread adoption of a new image of our fellow man and our relationship to him. . . . The most pervasive illness of our nation is loss of the guiding vision, and the cure is to be found in a nobler image of man and of a society in which his growth may be better nurtured.[92]

This enhanced self-image, this exalted image of man and his relationship to his fellowman, is what *The Stranger* proffers, bringing to this century the guiding vision of the Judeo-Christian tradition in new and meaningful terms—in the terms *of depth and growth psychology,* and a revival of the pioneering spirit of the West as men explore the unknown frontier of human consciousness and its development.

Harold could not have said it better than Harman—this nobler vision of man is the cure, more surely than vast social programs. It is essential if action on the social scene is to be sustained and efficacious. But Harold would have added to Harman's insights that there must also be the infusion of an exalted and affirmative image of the universe, because observations and empirical data do not warrant the nihilistic view that Science nurtures—and disaffection will persist for as long as such a view is held.

For example, Gerald Feinberg says, "I, therefore, think it time that scientists made it clear to others that the hypothesis of God is unnecessary within the scientific picture of the world. Those men who wish to retain their belief in God must recognize that none of the wide variety of phenomena revealed by the senses gives any support to their belief."[93]

We see here that scientists are willing to let everything in the universe evolve *but man's concept of God*. Religionists do not insist that Science be forever saddled with its outgrown conceptions. It has been nearly a century since the theology that views God as the bearded one in the sky collapsed. Today, God means the Cosmos and the energy operating within it in its every form. The concept of God cannot be less than Cosmic, universal, the whole situation and condition that scientists are dealing with.

To say that a hypothesis of God is unnecessary within the scientific picture is equivalent to saying that Science needs no cosmogony, no life sciences, no theory of light, space, particles, and that this condition of consciousness in an environment that communicates itself to our senses has no meaning. If so, there are no "long-range goals." Science cannot escape including in its picture a hypothesis of God, because the way Science views the universe *is* its hypothesis of God.

To say that the phenomena revealed by the *senses* fail to support belief is irrelevant. We do not taste, smell, touch, hear, or see a thought or self-consciousness that asks, "Who and what am I?" The phenomena revealed by exercise of mental energy do support the belief that understanding the universe and our part in it is primary. This is no more, no less, than an ongoing search for God. How exquisitely our senses support the belief that we are immersed in a *Supreme Reality* that expresses itself in countless ways—*and this reality is God*. Taste a loaf of bread, and you are tasting God. Feel the warmth of the sun, you are feeling God. See or hear what you will, you are seeing and hearing God.

The simple fact is that Religion and Science share the search for reality in all its depths, and the meaning inherent in man's ability to perceive it, even to the slightest degree. Therefore, they share the need for a new hypothesis of God, Cosmic Reality, and of man, the comprehender.

Today, forecasting the "shape" of society in the future has become a new science. The October 1968 and April 1969 issues of *The Futurist* carry articles by Burnham Beckwith, Robert Theobald, and others, discussing the changes that technology will bring.[94] Theobald is perceptive enough to see that a study of cybernetics demonstrates that technology will command of mankind the same ethical responses that Religion demands of humankind—in human terms: honesty, responsibility, love, and humility. Theobald says, "Cybernetics confirms religion as do the insights of those at the leading edge of almost all disciplines." Technology (mammon), too, serves God. Man is not to serve technology—it must serve him, his uniqueness in nature and as individual.

Remember this: Jesus did not decry nor despise mammon. He called mammon *unrighteous*, but he said that man was to *use mammon*—and he also said, "make to yourselves friends of the mammon of unrighteousness."[95] Why did he call mammon unrighteous?

Jesus saw that God and mammon form the "polarity" of Cosmic life. God—the remaining One, the WHOLE that is greater than the sum of its parts, is *righteous*. God, the righteous, is as nature's laws are: steadfast, unchanging, timeless. Mammon, the unrighteous, is as nature's energy is: volatile, constantly changing, and involved with time's action. Man is not to "serve" the energy; the energy is to serve him. Man is not to "serve" natural law; natural law is given to serve him. Natural law and the energy that operates according to its principles *cannot be separated*. To attempt to separate them into "two masters" is to try to separate God and nature or mind and matter. God and mammon are met in LIFE. Man is to serve life—his own, and all other. The question becomes, how best to serve life?

Theobald answers, "A single cultural norm is not necessary in the world of the future, rather we can expect great diversity. This point must be heavily stressed; it is one that Beckwith misses completely. He assumes a continuing process of homogenization of cultures despite the fact that the new dominant trend is toward the uniqueness of the individual and the diversity of cultures."

J. Blanton Belk, speaking of the future in *Pace Magazine*, says that the youth who participate in the "Up With People Sing Outs" are opening our eyes:

They will help us understand that the new order will come neither from technology nor politics nor even diplomacy, but much more from man himself, from a radical and permanent change in our way of thinking and our way of living.[96]

The views offered by *The Stranger* agree with this. But Harold did not decry technology. He saw it as the blessing that it is and will be. He saw also, however, that in man's understanding of himself and his natural powers rests even greater promise. As Religion evolves, "psychic technology" will also develop, bringing greater freedom *and* responsibility, because with each use of psi-power, man's conscious command of himself must be enlarged if the effect is to be lasting and beneficial.

SCENE III

Where Does Real Synthesis
Find a Place to Lay Its Head?

1) Son of man has no place to lay his head. Why?
2) How could Jesus have understood so much if he were not in some
way a "special" introduction into the human race? Was he the only
man to realize truth in such depth and magnitude?

To these questions, *The Stranger* answers as follows:

1) Jesus' doctrine was not his alone. It represented a *synthesis* of the
religious beliefs, thought, and knowledge of his day. Living at the crossroads of civilization, he had access to worldwide views and beliefs, even
if he never ventured out of Palestine. Synthesis, such as his teaching is,
evokes the synergistic force that is somehow greater than the force of
its component functions, of any one or all of them taken separately. It is
for this reason that real synthesis can find no place to lay its head. A new
structure large enough to house synergistic synthesis must evolve—and
this is an ongoing process.

2) Every human being who ever lived has the same capacity to realize
truth in all its depths as Jesus had. But not every person knows how
to tap this fount within himself and let the truth express itself through
his voice and deeds. Many men before Jesus knew how to tap this fount
—did, indeed, tap it to as great a degree as he did. But with each synthesis that brings together the sum of knowledge and experience, the
view is of wider dimension, because the knowledge and experience to
be incorporated is of wider dimension. And the vehicles of language and
mathematics that convey the realizations are more precise, enabling wider
meaning to be conveyed.

Jesus knew that synthesis would follow upon synthesis in time to come
—each surpassing the other and yet not invalidating it. He said that other
men would do greater deeds than he did. He knew that *a planetary con-*

127

cept of God and man would in time take over from the fragmented and divided religions. This would be the day when *the unity of God-consciousness in mankind would be recognized to be the basic factor to be considered in seeking truth.*

In order to reveal the dynamics of the psyche and its development, making himself a symbol of the Authority in man, Jesus could not state himself to be a "synthesizer," nor allow the symbol of Son of man to become involved with the personalities and lives of those from whom he drew, because in truth Son of man means the SELF, which is one, unique, only, in each human being.

But Jesus revealed that he strove for synthesis when he said that the day would come when all people would realize that worship of God, or expression of God-consciousness, would be valid only as it was done *in spirit and in truth* (John 4:24). This means: in a synthesis of intuition and intellect, in a synthesis of man's knowledge of the inner and outer realms of being, in a synthesis of world-wide religious expression and that intellectual accomplishment which we today call the sciences.

Harold takes such a giant step toward accomplishing this synthesis that *The Shining Stranger* may be considered to be *A New Testament for Our Times.*

The old concepts of God are dead or dying. They were slain by Science and Marxism, by the secular philosophers and the radical theologians. But Godless existentialism, scientific or otherwise, is now being hissed off the stage by a generation that somehow understands, even if it cannot yet articulate its belief, that there is within each person "something unearthly" which he must communicate to every soul on this planet, and to the stars. There is an Authority within him that prohibits his being a mere creature, or creature of anyone who has ever lived, or creature of any State. This generation says, "Love!"

And *The Stranger* replies, "Love forever remains the most daring answer to universal mystery. . . . Love is the answer to the mystery of nature, of life, of God, that Jesus gave."[97]

If Western religions are going to have a place in the *Synthesis of God-consciousness* that tomorrow's Religion must be, they must transcend their Messianic claims and expectations by *internalizing* the Messianic ideal and developing it along psychological lines. The sacred writings of each of the religions must be studied anew in the light of modern knowledge, which keeps catching up with the legendary truth of the Scriptures, and with Jesus' poetic words, and with the first and most piercing insight of Mohammed:

128

Read! For thy Lord is most beneficent
Who hath taught the use of the pen;
Hath taught man that which he knew not.[98]

Nothing in nature knew the "use of the pen," nothing in nature could teach it to man. Only "thy Lord," the Authority within him, vesting him with God-power and God-consciousness, could accomplish this.

If this generation would seek a frame of reference within which it may measure its grasp of the inward Authority in man and come to understand its psychic functions, it may study the words and lives of the great religious figures in human history. Each is a prototype, each confirms the other, each insists that holiness is to be identified with the divinely human, each says man is uniquely an expression of the Divine Mind through which the Cosmos took form.

Today, if the Gospels are studied in the light of modern knowledge, Jesus' *own words* show that—well, let *The Stranger* say it:

Jesus presented Himself *as* Messiah must present himself to fulfill the role as it was described in Scriptures, the frame in which and against which Messiah could be measured. He chose this way to show the "truth of truth": it finishes itself always in cross-action which demands a change-over and reconciles opposites by reflecting the confronting image as likeness. Likeness is all that can be perceived.

In finishing the Judaic Messianic role by playing it to its bitter end, He broke the mold and any like unto it. Judaic-Messiah came into the world in the Bible, made manifold in the one volume encompassing the expression of Homo sapiens' consciousness. Until Judaism reborn in Christianity had been presented to the East, to which Jesus acknowledged His debt in His birth legend, mankind could not be relieved of false Messianic expectation by coming to see that the same truth is expressed in every religion. . . .

Truth—what is truth? Each man who seeks life's profound mystery long enough, diligently enough, comes finally to say, "I am truth." . . . Jesus' teaching leads man to grasp truth, the Christ-being, in another and in all others, for until a man has done so he cannot sustain in sanity the knowledge of the Christ-being within himself as he becomes aware of its truth and power.

This need to see Christ-being in another can be met only by preserving the religions that enfold symbols of God incarnate in man. Jesus recognized the need to preserve the mother-church even as the tissue of the new religious idea is given shape and form. . . .

What is God? Jesus said: God is *love*. Love is the mystery that gives meaning to life, *the force of attraction that binds in imperishable union all in creation from the "least" particle, the neutrino, to the universe it-self, and every precious relationship within it. . . .* Jesus said: God is *spirit*. Spirit is unmanifest, save as the unmeasurable energy of mind, and of space itself. Jesus said: God is the *word*. The power of the word, of speech, is now expressed by man, although he cannot define it, or discern its dynamics, or calculate its limits.

Jesus taught that in the power of the word rests the creative principle which insures the enlightenment of man, and the becoming of the universe to express the ideal in being and change that sustains life and satisfaction in life.

He taught that God, "The Absolute," gave itself into nature and man, thereby destroying "The Absolute" in life's operation wherein power is shared with man and expressed in the working of perfect natural law through which truth reigns and governs.

Jesus taught that through the working of natural law, God works. He showed and taught, however, that within natural law the "miraculous" is possible—as is evidenced in phenomena arising from hypnosis, *and* in the miracles wrought when man seeks truth, applies knowledge in the natural realm, and operates the ethic of love and honesty in dealing with mammon.

Jesus taught that truth and God-power are perfectly divided, perfectly stated, in "one," each as "I," and in the principle *one* enfolds: *one* is absolute unto itself only, is indestructible, inexhaustible. God is One-Parent-Being with life in itself which cannot be *objectified*, save as the universe and all within it, because this One-Parent-Being is *subjectified* in man, Son, who thereby has everlasting life in himself and in whom is reserved one power no other creature expresses: word-power.

It is the Father-Son relationship between God and man that brings love to life, brings moments of joy complete, brings moments of peace that passeth understanding, brings quiet confidence in the grace of nature and of God.[99]

Jesus saw that the seed of God that man bears within him will come to flower if man but sleeps and rises—but just as nature brings with each cycle a fruition that must be harvested and resown to produce greater abundance, so in the many lives man lives he harvests the understanding that has come to him. Thy Lord, seed of God man bears within him, "will not suffer thy foot to be moved. . . . The Lord shall preserve thee from all evil: he shall preserve thy soul. The Lord shall preserve thy going out and thy coming in from this time forth, and even for ever-more."[100] You will not lose what you have gained in understanding. You and nature will be preserved from the *absolute* or "all evil." Your soul is made of all you have known of love and satisfaction, and from life to life it is preserved in the kingdom within. Your life is eternal, ever-lasting; even though you "go out," you "come in" again. The more you mature in consciousness the more evenly this transition occurs, until it becomes in time like breathing. Self-union, whole-being associated with whole-being, consciousness that resonates perfectly with the Cosmic con-sciousness of God, will someday express itself in humankind, who will have then conquered death.

"Come now, let us reason together, saith the Lord . . ."—and this is what Harold says to the religions, to the sciences, and to the contesting political ideologies.[101] The *Synthesis* that will command man's faith, the Religion of tomorrow, must encompass all knowledge and experience. Only then can the continuous cross-action between intellect and intui-tion, between desire and practicality, work through the evolutionary process to make society anew, and proffer a faith that warrants belief because it accords with all that man knows of reality. Such a faith will invite its own further development. When the principles of such a faith are stated, *practice supported by belief* will bring on action that is real —action that will give our "planetary being" a unified human soul as well as a "world brain" that will lead mankind toward self-government under law, evolving always to meet society's needs. *The Shining Stranger* proffers the unifying principles upon which such a faith may base itself.

How can this "Celestial Child" be other than schizophrenic if a part of its mind is consumed with fear that it is a dying body in a dying host? Some millions of years are but as a watch in the night to Planet Earth. Its *human mind* can leap ahead in time and experience the condition of cold, senseless chaos.

How can this "Celestial Child" pull its wits together if half its brain thinks that it is no more than an animal, and the other half thinks it is God? Who will tell it that it is neither—it is divine material made human and habitable for life? What can life mean to it if with half its thinking it sees its own particular life of no more value than an insect's, here today, forever gone tomorrow—and with the other half of thinking it concludes that it is to live forever in heaven or hell, or in an endless chain of death and birth which leads to nothing? Why should it try to correct its ways if there is no purpose, no goal, no becoming in its journey through the sunlit days and starry evenings? Can you imagine the terror of a living child, ready for birth, encased in the womb of a dead or dying body?

Today, our "Celestial Child," Planet Earth, is encased in the sac of the body of belief which is dead or dying—and yet envelops the globe.

Someone must perform a Caesarean that will give the *individual and the universe* a living principle from which to draw the breath of life. Harold has done this. *The Shining Stranger* speaks to the principle of life vested in the individual, giving every life purpose and meaning. But *The Stranger* cannot speak to the principle of the living universe because this part of Harold's work was not included in that book. We will deal with it in *If Thine Eye Be Single.*

Here, we must admit that the final answer to the Palestinian mystery play cannot, of course, be given. *The attempt to give a final answer has been the trouble in the past.*

Christianity insisted that St. Paul had given the final answer. *The Stranger* says that St. Paul gave the best answer that could be given according to the light of his day, and he dealt magnificently with his own generation—better than could the "children of light," the disciples. But it would take time to reveal the real meaning of Jesus—and time is revealing it. Messianic expectation, Judaic or Christian or Islamic, can be realized only in a subjective way: looking for an objectified Messiah is like looking for a final answer or final truth. There *is no finality in truth —and this is why life and the universe are everlasting.*

Harold accomplished such a monumental synthesis that there is no place for it to lay its head—not in any one or all of the religions combined, not in any of today's temples of the various sciences and psychologies, not in the confines of any ideology. If it could fit into any of these places neatly, it would not be real synthesis. And it is.

Oliver Reiser has also accomplished real synthesis in his philosophy of Cosmic Humanism. The reach and scope of his work is such that there is no specific structure to contain it. Therefore, it may well become the framework with sufficient dimension to shelter the emergent planetary concept of man, as well as God-consciousness now expressing itself in terms of Cosmic consciousness.

Bringing together Harold's and Reiser's syntheses produces greater synthesis than either author has produced alone. Reiser could bring to this union something that Harold did not. That is, the name to house tomorrow's living principle, which is what Religion is: Cosmic Humanism.

Again, it must be pointed out that Harold did not once use the word *humanism.* He may have refrained from doing so because humanism is associated with atheism or "heartless" scientism by so many people. Today, there are religious and nonreligiously oriented humanists. It is fitting to associate Harold's work with Cosmic Humanism only if we see that in this name we have a modern translation of "God is love."

$$\text{Cosmos} = \text{God}$$
$$\text{Humanism} = \text{Love}$$

Love is made of understanding. Therefore, it must embrace all knowledge and experience.

Cosmic Humanism, which actually began with God-consciousness coming into expression in man, must continue to be what it has always been: an ongoing synthesis of the light of humankind—man and the planet operating as symbiotic bodies within the universe, guided in their development toward an optimum state of being by the mind and eye of God.

Epilogue

After this day, July 20, 1969, can man express less than Cosmic consciousness? Can he express less than his divine humanity as he treats with his fellowman? Men walked upon the moon, all the while conversing with men upon the earth, and the world watched.

But something more than this happened. Something far more important. Planet Earth, our Celestial Child, thought its *first coherent thought*. Simultaneously, and all over the globe, millions of its mental cells—human minds—had but one concern, one desire. *One image only was acting upon this concerted consciousness.* The World Sensorium must have sent into the universe wave-trains of mental energy that may fall upon some distant receptor and shape the words which in any tongue speak the message the planet transmitted in full force: God give victory to our astronauts and bring them safely home.

One will, *one* wish, *one* exultation cohered the minds of people the world over, and therefore the mind of this earth. All that divides us was forgotten—must it be again remembered?—in those magnificent hours when for the first time in human history so many *simultaneously sent forth goodwill toward man.* Toward *man*, who in some dim past had emerged a creature from sea deeps, now to keep his first rendezvous with life's rich promise: "dust thou art and unto dust shalt thou return"—to stand upon a sea of glittering moon dust and speak to the universe in the name of humankind.

The earth was hushed and holy—wholly involved in the dream and in the *reality* of its fulfillment.

More than a new age was born in this magnetic moment—a moment that must resonate with that long-ago magnetic moment when the first aquatic creature "walked" of its own accord from water to explore dry land. A new consciousness stirred in the unified mind of *humankind*.

Empathy, global, drew the viewers and the actors into harmonious union as they shared the anxiety and experienced the triumph our species had worked from its beginning to achieve. Where do we begin giving praise? Who lit the first fire, shaped the first wheel?

Our generation is the first to reap a space harvest. And ours is the first generation to hear Planet Earth cease for a moment to babble fretfully. It spoke as with one voice: "I am the body that has borne man, dreamer of Cosmic dreams, doer of Cosmic deeds, and never more human, more divine, than in this moment of power and glory when his heart is humble, when awe falls like dew upon his mind."

While *Apollo XI* was visiting the moon, was not earth actually broadcasting its first comprehensible message into space? This, because, for the first time in history, there may have been sufficient mental energy perfectly focused and intensely concentrated to resonate as one voice sending a powerful and clarion call of goodwill toward the stars.

We do not know whether there are ears elsewhere to hear. Never mind, Humankind gets the message: man will occupy new spheres—new spheres of consciousness, and new spheres in the universe. And, if we are alone in the Cosmos, *The Stranger* says:

> . . . in some very distant tomorrow, man's destiny may be to "Be fruitful, and multiply, and replenish" the "many mansions" to be found in space. . . .
>
> As to the question of how to live in this world or in the universe, it is not possible to present a new answer that will surpass the highest and most practical ethic of Homo sapiens—his consciousness cannot rise above the ethic of love, enfolded in the Golden Rule which is given in all of the world's great religions. Although this, man's light, may be as little as the firefly casts, nevertheless, it is to be regarded as India's great poet, Rabindranath Tagore, regarded the firefly's: his light may be tiny, but it is not small, for it is akin to all the light in the universe. Someday, Homo sapiens may bring light to mansions far flung in space—for:
>
> Neither do men light a candle, and put it under a bushel, but on a candlestick; and it giveth light unto all that are in the house.[102]

We may yet catch a ray from the reflector man put upon the moon—the first candle he has set to light our solar house.

On earth, we see in the morning newspapers that as always people are saying yes and no to everything that pertains to the space program. Many insist that tax money would have been better spent salving our social wounds. An Indian tribe protested, saying that to them the moon is sacred, and now it has been defiled. But even while clucking concern, something in the heart of every man is saying, "Still higher, ever upward —Excelsior!" It is as though the earth itself knows that on this, the day of man's visit to the moon, the mind of humankind struck the lost chord, and the voice of the planet soared into the night.

"A U M . . . heaven . . ."

On the jacket of the record, *The Moody Blues in Search of the Lost Chord*, we read, "The most important word of power in the Hindu scriptures is the word *OM*, which pronounced A U M means 'God,' 'All,' 'Being,' 'The answer' . . ."[103] Did you, by chance, listen to Mike Pinder's song, *OM*, as Eagle sat on the moon?

Have you seen the special issue of *Pace Magazine*, devoted to space, and come upon the picture of Dr. Viktor Frankl, mountain climbing, commenting, "Man goes beyond necessities to the very limits of possibilities because he wonders where those limits lie. And behold, they don't lie anywhere because like the horizon, they expand with every step he takes toward them."[104] In the same issue, Igor Sikorsky, speaking of the possibilities of space travel, made a daring remark, "I venture to make the totally heretical statement—from the standpoint of modern science —that the velocity of light is not the limit of velocity. Much greater velocities can exist in the universe even though we have never observed them and cannot imagine them."[105] Well, Preston Harold ventured to say the same thing. He described this "Q-force" in *On the Nature of Universal Cross-Action* and saw that it must exist and will be used to trace a royal road to the stars.

Man has increased the speed at which his vehicles can travel until now the sound barrier has been broken. As he thinks of venturing far into space, even the speed of light seems insufficient, if he could actually travel at this rate, as time is measured by our life span. We must break the "light barrier" before travel into distant space becomes practical. Or, we could say that such space travel cannot be accomplished until complete consciousness produces the incorruptible flesh that will permit everlasting life, so that the "time barrier" will be broken. Or can we stretch our minds to think upon the "speed of darkness" as opposed to the "speed of light"? If the Q-force flows through space, as Harold envisions, is it possible to break the "light barrier" and travel at the speed of "dark" energy—a speed at which, in Harold's view, matter takes shape and might hold its form? The question is dizzying, but it must be asked. And among the barriers we must break are mental barriers—those born of Religion and Science. We must seek to achieve everlasting life in robust health, not for the purpose of eternal harp playing, but in order to fulfill our destiny of exploring space—if this be our destiny. We must seek through Science to tap the power of unmanifest energy, the "dark," as well as of manifest energy, the light. Which is to say, scientists must learn how to call upon the manifest *and* the unmanifest power in man and the universe that we call God.

And, now, please turn to Act One, Scene I, "The Premise," upon which this Play takes its stand, leaving the verdict to you, the jury of readers. Will you agree that the "Moon Scene" in the Drama of Man makes our point for us: Humankind is chalice of the power of God, and is destined to have dominion over nature's realm—the dominion that understanding brings—just as Adam was told by the God-consciousness that opened his eyes to behold the world in the beginning of the Palestinian mystery play.

References

References for this edition, excerpted from The Single Reality, *begin with Number 4.*

THE PALESTINIAN MYSTERY PLAY
Act One: Setting the Stage for *The Shining Stranger*

4 Preston Harold, *The Shining Stranger* (New York: Dodd, Mead & Co., distributors; Wayfarer Press, publishers, 1967).

5 Henry Miller; see comments on the jacket cover of *The Shining Stranger*.

6 Attributed to Oscar Wilde, source unknown.

7 Oliver L. Reiser, *Cosmic Humanism* (Cambridge, Mass.: Schenkman Publishing Co., 1966).

8 William Shakespeare, *Hamlet*, Act II, sc. 2, l. 632.

9 Montague Rhodes James, translator, The Apocryphal New Testament (Oxford, England: The Clarendon Press, 1966), pp. 49, 50.

10 Luke 2:46-47.

11 I. Rice Pereira, *The Transcendental Formal Logic of the Infinite: The Evolution of Cultural Forms* (New York: Pereira, 1966), pp. 4, 5.

12 James, Gospel of Thomas, The Apocryphal New Testament, p. 51.

13 *I Ching (The Book of Changes)* Wilhelm-Baynes tr, (New York: Pantheon, 1950).

14 Ernest Renan, *The Life of Jesus* (New York: Random House, Modern Library, 1927), p. 386.

15 Attributed to Will Durant.

16 I Cor. 6:20, 7:23.

17 Matt. 5:13-14, 25:40; John 10:34-35, 8:32.

18 Robert L. Heilbroner, *The Worldly Philosophers* (New York: Simon & Schuster, 1961), p. 126.

19 Nikita Khrushchev, Associated Press Release, San Francisco, September 22, 1959.

20 Carl G. Jung, *Man and His Symbols* (New York: Doubleday, 1964), p. 261.

21 Luke 12:15; Matt. 4:4, 6:25.

22 Gerald Holton, "Science and New Styles of Thought," *Thirtieth Anniversary Lecture Series* (University College, University of Florida, University College Series, No. 1, May, 1967), p. 17.

23 Rudolf Thiel, *And There Was Light* (New York: Alfred A. Knopf, 1967), p. 336.

24 Krishnamurti, "Conversation," *Journal* (Claremont, Calif.: The Blaisdell Institute, Vol. IV, No. 1, January, 1969), p. 23.

25 Harold, *The Shining Stranger*, pp. 304, 305.

26 *Ibid.*, p. 319.

27 Lord Byron, *Childe Harold's Pilgrimage* (London, England: John Murray, 1818), Canto IV, CXXXVII, p. 71.

28 Harold, *The Shining Stranger*, pp. 380, 383.

Act Two: *The Shining Stranger* Speaks

29 Harold, *The Shining Stranger*, p. 22.

30 *Ibid.*, p. 104.

31 *Equals One* (Pondicherry, India: Auroville, 1968), "The Take-Off," p. 86.

32 Abraham Maslow, *Psychology Today* (July, 1968).

33 Harold, *The Shining Stranger*, pp. 300, 301.

34 *Ibid.*, p. 298.

35 *Ibid.*, p. 305.

36 Micah 4:5.

37 Harold, *The Shining Stranger*, p. 393.

38 *Ibid.*, pp. 29, 30, 31.

39 John 14:26.

40 Matt. 26:64.

41 Matt. 24:35.

42 John 5:21, 3:1-7.

43 John 12:48, 5:22.

44 Harold, *The Shining Stranger*, pp. 328, 329.

45 Matt. 24:36, 42, 44, 50.

46 Matt. 24:4-5, 23-26.

47 Willis W. Harman, "Old Wine in New Wineskins," in *Challenges of Humanistic Psychology*, James F. T. Bugental, ed. (New York: McGraw-Hill, 1967), Chapter 33, p. 322.

48 Harold, *The Shining Stranger*, Chapters 11 through 15. (In the discussion of the miracles, individual references will be omitted because the large number to be given would be distracting to the reader. See Index of the book.)

49 Dr. H. A. Puharich, 432 W. 45th St., New York, N.Y.

50 *The Graduate*, Columbia Masterworks, Stereo OS 3180, record-jacket copy by Charles Burr.

51 Harold, *The Shining Stranger*, pp. 316-319, 332.

52 Cyril Greenland, "Richard Maurice Bucke, *Can. Med. Asso. Jour.*, M.D., 1837-1902," 91 (1964) 385-391, quoting Bucke's *Cosmic Consciousness*.

53 Mark 15:34.

54 John 19:34.

55 Harold, *The Shining Stranger*, pp. 313, 314.

[56] *Ibid.*, pp. 314, 315, 316.
[57] *Ibid.*, p. 336.
[58] *Ibid.*, pp. 166-170.
[59] *Ibid.*, pp. 50-55.
[60] *Ibid.*, pp. 82-85.
[61] Mark 10:18.
[62] Harold, *The Shining Stranger*, p. 111.
[63] *Ibid.*, p. 136 (See also p. 112 and Chapter 6).
[64] Matt. 6:33-34.
[65] Matt. 7:1-2.
[66] John 15:13-14.
[67] Clifford P. Owens, *A Story of Jesus* (Virginia Beach, Va.: A. R. E. Press, 1963), based on the Edgar Cayce readings. Also, James E. Padgett, *True Gospel Revealed Anew by Jesus*, 3rd ed. (Washington, D.C.: Church of the New Birth, 1965).
[68] Matt. 24:5.
[69] Mark 9:41.
[70] *Wall Street Journal*, September 1969. Article headlined: "Bible Sales Fall off as Religion's Influence on Americans Dwindles."

Act Three: Truth Is the Shining Stranger Mankind Seeks

[71] Harold, *The Shining Stranger*, p. 386.
[72] *Ibid.*, Chapters 6 through 9.
[73] *Ibid.*, p. 210.
[74] Ira Progoff, *Depth Psychology and Modern Man* (New York: Julian Press, 1959), pp. 215-219.
[75] I. S. Bengelsdorf, "Man Not the Only Toolmaker, Scholar Says," *Los Angeles Times*, Feb. 23, 1969, p. C1, quoting Leakey.
[76] Harold, *The Shining Stranger*, pp. 386, 387.
[77] *Ibid.*, p. 371.
[78] *Ibid.*, p. 303.
[79] *Ibid.*, pp. 51, 52, 53, 67.
[80] *Ibid.*, p. 58.
[81] *Ibid.*, p. 379.
[82] Mark 8:36.
[83] Harold, *The Shining Stranger*, pp. 348, 369.
[84] *Ibid.*, p. 362.
[85] Stuart Palmer, *Science News* 95 (1969), 356.
[86] Harold, *The Shining Stranger*, p. 347.
[87] *Ibid.*, p. 361.
[88] *Ibid.*, p. 346.

[89] *Ibid.*, p. 370.

[90] *Ibid.*, pp. 365, 362.

[91] *Ibid.*, pp. 376-379.

[92] Willis W. Harman, "The New Copernican Revolution," *Stanford Today*, Winter, 1969, p. 8.

[93] Joel A. Snow, "Taking Thought for the Morrow" (book review), *Science*, Vol. 164, 18 April 1969, p. 285.

[94] Robert Theobald, "Alternative Methods of Predicting the Future," *The Futurist*, Vol. iii, No. 2 (Washington, D.C.: World Future Society), April, 1969. See also: "Beckwith's Reply to Robert Theobald," pp. 43-46.

[95] Luke 16:9-13.

[96] J. Blanton Belk, "Man's Gotta Go Somewhere," a *Pace Magazine* reprint (Los Angeles, Calif., 835 So. Flower St., 1969), p. 3.

[97] Harold, *The Shining Stranger*, p. 392.

[98] *Ibid.*, p. 274.

[99] *Ibid.*, pp. 382-394.

[100] Ps. 121:8.

[101] Harold, *The Shining Stranger*, p. 208.

[102] *Ibid.*, pp. 386, 387.

[103] Mike Pinder, "OM," London Records, Inc. (New York) Stereo Des 18019, 1968.

[104] Geoffrey Frost, "The Cosmos and the Mind: A dialogue with Viktor Frankl," *Pace Magazine*, Vol. V, No. 8 (August, 1969), p. 36.

[105] John Sayre, "I Have Dreamed about It All My Life: A talk with helicopter inventor, Igor Sikorsky," *Pace Magazine*, Vol. V, No. 8 (August, 1969), p. 31.